cannondale
cannondale
cannondale

VELO
2ND GEAR

BICYCLE
CULTURE
AND
STYLE

gestalten

PRE-FACE

BY SHONQUIS MORENO

Once upon a time, in about 3600 BC, someone pegged a set of wheels to a cart; 4,400 years later, the roads of Baghdad were finally paved with tar. But it wasn't until 1817 that German Baron Karl Drais von Sauerbronn put two wheels beneath a simple seat. Two hundred years later, the bicycle represents one of the most efficient ways on earth to transform man power into movement, converting up to 99% of leg motion and allowing a rider to pedal over 1,000 kilometers on the energy equivalent of one liter of petrol. And consider this: Today, emissions from car exhaust kill more people than crashes do and bikes certainly move faster than congested traffic. Happily then, bike aesthetics and technology are advancing rapidly and with a gratifying eclecticism and, like so many other possessions, have become expressions of who we are and who we would like to be. Of course, for all these reasons, bikes are political too, sparking bitter debates about anything from sports ethics and women's emancipation to global warming, healthcare, and urban planning.

TOKYOBIKE pages 40–43

Above all, however, bikes are both the subject and object of one of the richest and increasingly pervasive international subcultures of the day. Even while the professional racing world absorbs hard truths about doping following the stripping of Lance Armstrong's Tour de France titles, the passion for every kind of cycling is blazing. And not just in Copenhagen, Europe's longstanding bicycling capital or in the Netherlands, where even as early as the 1970s, the government was footing the bill for 80% of the country's urban biking infrastructure. Since 2000, bike commuting has increased by over 70% in major US cities while in Portland, Oregon, which has become the poster child of the American cycling nation, it has exploded by over 250%. But if it is a culture that is growing, it is also a culture whose codes, aesthetics, and dedication have diversified and deepened, a trend that has found roots and recovered its sophistication. In brief: it is a culture that has been growing up.

When Baron von Sauerbronn built his wood, brass, and iron *Laufmaschine* (running machine), he built it for collecting taxes from his tenants and, sadly for them, was able to cover more than 13 km an hour in doing so. His steerable, pedalless, person-powered vehicle was called a draisine or draisienne, its two wheels set in-line to create something like a kid's balance bike. Which makes it apt that, though the cartwrights who produced them awkwardly dubbed them "pedestrian curricles," the public referred to them as hobby or dandy-horses, like the child's toy. Indeed, the rider pushed alternately with one foot and then the other—being, in effect, the horse. In the 1860s, riders of the French *vélocipède*, with its rotary cranks and pedals (the derailleur arrived 40 years later) began at last to call it a "bicycle."

Since then the bicycle has come a long way. In the following pages, we will be introduced to the increasingly far-flung bicycle family, no longer a diaspora, but a gene fragment that has spread without borders. These are disparate but sometimes overlapping tribes who share common attitudes to issues and similar penchants for gear, host their own events finally began and surmount their own particular geographies, but who are all committed to making bicycling a part of their multidimensional lives. Multidimensional because, increasingly, biking and bike design are being done not just by bike pros, but by industrial designers, architects, would-be mechanical geeks, aerospace engineers, and amateurs at home with a hex key who have all caught the bug. People who once had nothing in common are using the bike to commute and to trek, to launch planet-friendly businesses, and build formal or informal cycling networks and organizations that bring a spectrum of personalities and purposes together. Today, while these laymen find that their lives are more about bikes, the pros are insisting that their lives are about more than just bikes—a sign that what may once have been merely a trend has become entrenched in mainstream culture.

THE CITY

Everywhere, but especially in dense metropolises, bike culture rides right into political issues that affect city planning, sustainability, public health, and mobility (or a lack of all of these): The couriers may remain a fiercely independent and high-profile tribe, but urban bicyclists have many faces today. They are building bikes from whatever materials they have at hand, giving passers-by the spectacle of high bikes and lowriders, and liberating urbanites who would otherwise be stuck at a dead-stop on subway platforms and bored to death in bus queues.

Since 2011, New York has devoted miles of green paint to the creation of a network of more than 200 bike lanes (wonderful), but has failed to keep them clear for use by bikers (less wonderful). To protest being fined $50 by New York City for not riding in the bike lane, filmmaker Casey Neistat shot a video demonstrating what would happen to any biker who unflinchingly did so—crashing repeatedly into construction equipment, taxis, moving trucks, sink holes, double-parked cars, and even a police car—and then posted it on YouTube where it has almost six million views in just over a year.

New York is not alone in its challenges. Even in the mid-19th century, velocipedes were causing a fracas: Crashes were considerably less forceful back then, but much like today, since bicycles were often operated on the smooth sidewalk instead of rough roads, cities began to outlaw them or charge fines for infractions. Those rough rides were harshest in England and America, however, where riders had renamed the innocent hobby horse, the "boneshaker," because its rigid frame and iron-band wheels made the ride bone-rattling (a problem diminished with the introduction of ball bearings and solid rubber tires). By now, we have the comfort of Swedish studio Hövding's Invisible Bicycle Helmet: an inconspicuous collar that inflates during a collision. An algorithm controls battery-powered sensors that monitor the wearer's movement and signal a helium gas inflator if they detect any extraordinary motion.

BIKES ARE ONE OF THE RICHEST AND INCREASINGLY PERVASIVE INTERNATIONAL SUBCULTURES OF THE DAY

ELIANCYCLES
pages 128–130

Today it is from the cities that some of the most creative remedies have emerged: bicycle share programs that came out of the bike-savvy Netherlands and France in the 1960s and 1970s and new platforms like Liquid, an online network of private individuals offering personal bikes for place-based rental. There are spontaneous people-powered solutions too: during Hurricane Sandy, while power and transit were down in lower Manhattan, a group of riders organized "bike trains" to drop people off at their offices. In 2012, the grassroots bike advocacy group Critical Mass—ignited by a leaderless group ride in San Francisco and turned into an "organized coincidence" that occurs on the last Friday of every month in cities around the world—celebrated its 20th anniversary.

To keep pace with the quickening city and perhaps to amplify the risk inherent to urban living, couriers designed fixies from track bikes. Now, hybrid bicycles like the Mixie have become popular, mixing fixed gear with road-friendliness and sophisticated looks. On the other hand, Tokyobikes, originally designed for the space-starved Japanese and for comfort over speed, are meant to help slow life down, making the journey the destination.

Also addressing lack of space, British studio Eyetohand's Contortionist bicycle features a frame that folds to fit between its wheels, its chain drive replaced with an internal hydraulic system. Another prototype by Brit Duncan Fitzsimons even boasts wheels that fold up with the frame to create the most compact carriage yet proposed. Urban portage issues are attended to with cargo bikes like Elian Veltman's Dutch designs that lighten the city load by transporting groceries, children, and goods, alike.

FASHION & IDENTITY

Today's bike fashions—with their savvier attention to color, cut, and material—embrace both the prêt a porter and the haute couture. The chic set, who may have dipped into bikes not so long ago because they were trendy and fashion-forward, are now becoming experts, addicts, and converts. This group lives at the crossroads of self-expression, creativity, and cool, where bike culture overlaps with design and aesthetics. The style clergy look both forward and back in time to define themselves and their place in the world, and the result of their focus on cycling is an exploding panoply of sometimes overwhelming and sometimes subdued graphics, iconography, color schemes, branding, and obsessive detailing that wrap tubes, are carved into saddles, or woven amongst wheel spokes today. Like trainers and toothbrushes, the bike frame and its accessories are often overdesigned, yes, but the finest work—like Brooks' worked-leather saddles by Kara Ginther or its picnic pannier, which could have been made for Louis Vuitton—is very fine indeed. Even mass personalization by the likes of Sweden's BIKEID with its 10,000-plus color combinations and its emphasis on involving the rider in the creation of his ride or, Bike by Me with its online "configurator," churns out its beauties.

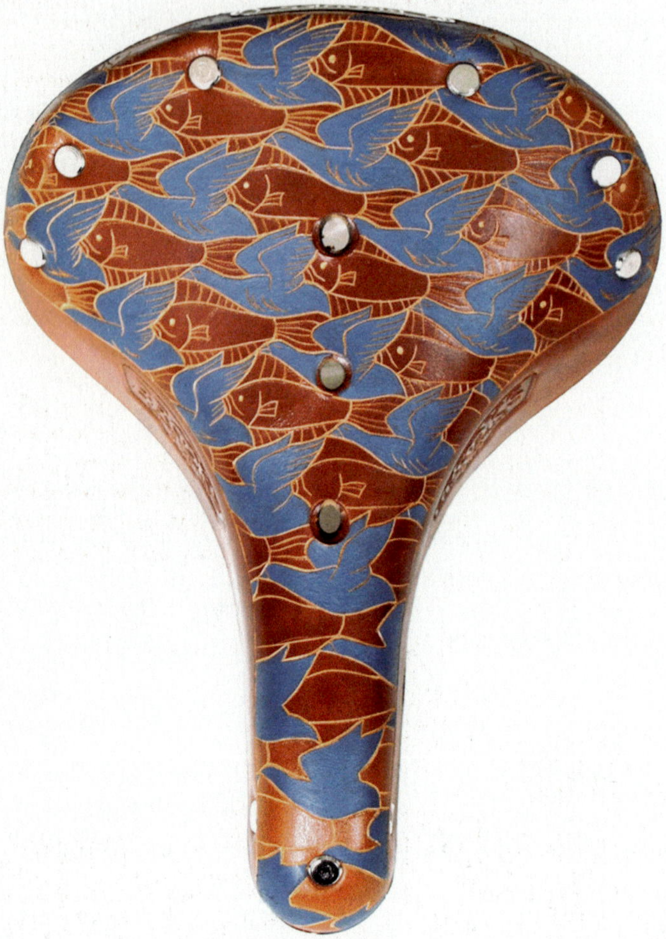

KARA GINTHER page 38

In effect, this means that custom frames and mass-customized bikes are the new accessories, themselves. No longer the sole domain of hardcore riders, they appeal to hipsters, fashionistas, and city dwellers for whom personalization is an articulation of identity along with that of their headphones, smart phones, and sneakers.

By now, there are accessories for the home and those for the body of the bike and its rider. Quarterre makes bike racks in walnut veneer or folded steel that accommodate bikes in homes where bike storage never used to be an issue—as artistry to be hung on the walls. South Korea's Yeongkeun Jeong and Aareum Jeong created Reel, an elastic band attached with silicone dots and wrapped repeatedly between the tubes to carry belongings and baguettes. In Peru, a French designer's fashion label, Misericordia, collaborated with Abici Bicycles to reinterpret the draisienne bicycle. He also designed jackets and polo shirts to accompany his Velocino.

Reinterpretations may be skin-deep, others recall something deeper. Vanguard's Churchill bicycle has an enlarged front wheel and small rear. It is a latter-day penny farthing, which was first designed by Frenchman Eugene Meyer and was all the rage for a couple of decades from the 1860s, but the enlarged wheel increased speed while, unfortunately, decreasing safety. This meant that, bound as they were by Victorian mores (and whalebone stays), women didn't get much pedal time in until the arrival of the "safety bicycle" in the 1890s, which turned a dangerous plaything for younger men into a practical tool for the daily transport of both sexes.

Suffragist Susan B. Anthony called it the "freedom machine," saying that the bicycle had "done more to emancipate women than anything else in the world," and women—accoutered in progressive "rational" fashions that threw off the corset and ankle-length skirt for bloomers—flocked to it. By 1895, activist Frances Willard would find herself using a biking metaphor to incite her followers to action: "I would not waste my life in friction," she told them, "when it could be turned into momentum."

TECHNOLOGY: PLAYHORSES & WORKHORSES

Today, of course, technology is very much in fashion. Bikers and designers are pushing technology to its limit while others let it push them to theirs. Techie creatives have lightened, strengthened, and streamlined frames, components, and gear to an extreme, improving performance by precious milliseconds. To do so, they use tools like computer-aided design, finite element analysis, and computational fluid dynamics. Computer simulations help test designs while hydroforming and automated carbon fiber layup produce them. Some manufacturers, like German brand Canyon, even keep a CT scanner on hand and 3D-print their prototypes.

On-bike, at its best, technology is rendered invisible beneath beveled tubes, pretty leather picnic baskets, and lace-up calfskin handlebars. Electronic gadgetry has proliferated—and then disappeared: to cyclocomputers, manufacturers now add cycling power meters and electronic gear-shifting systems. A team of mechanical engineering students at the University of Pennsylvania created the "integrated systems" Alpha bike with an enclosed belt drive, an electronically controlled clutch that switches between fixed gear and freewheeling and, in the handlebars, an LCD display that captures cycling statistics on an SD card.

TECHIE CREATIVES HAVE LIGHTENED, STRENGTHENED, AND STREAMLINED FRAMES, COMPONENTS, AND GEAR TO AN EXTREME, IMPROVING PERFORMANCE

In the 1970s and 1980s, due to a shrinking European steel industry, a booming Asian market, and the widening use of TIG welding, many brands turned away from steel frames towards durable but relatively lightweight aluminum, titanium, and carbon. (That said, not all efforts to bring new materials and techniques into the industry met with success: In the 80s, Swedish brand Itera launched a bicycle made entirely of plastic—it was a huge retail failure.)

Technological innovations have produced and perfected the playhorses and workhorses of the biking world from trekking bikes that can race around the world to extreme terrain bikes by aerospace engineer Dan Hanebrink, and mountain and touring bikes that help riders escape city life into the great outdoors, for extreme sport or just to travel.

Lately, however, we find ourselves sometimes pushing aside the "high" technology: Although it is relatively manual and low-tech, the Speedmax Evo has the highly advanced capacity to let riders make small sliding adjustments to components that shift the bike into over 7500 configurations, as if tailoring their own clothes. We are also returning to organic materials like bamboo or wood as Andy Martin did to create his curlicued bent beechwood road bicycle for Thonet. At other times, we're using whatever materials we can find at hand: Tristan Kopp's ProdUser is a kit of only four components connected by their users via found materials and turned into a low-tech and locally made bike.

CLASSICS & THE CONNOISSEURS

It is the classic cyclists that keep the best of bicycling history and values alive. A fondness for vintage gear, cycles, and lifestyles has to do not just with style, but more profoundly with a particular brand of dedication and ideals. Classicists are a passionate lot, with a devotion to craftsmanship, sportsmanship, and (obsessive) detail.

The recent surge in framebuilding has paralleled a mainstream resurgence in many crafts in reaction to the info-saturated, LCD-illuminated digital existence we lead today. There is a rational elegance in mechanical devices that are what they look like, with every connection visible, and that almost anyone can learn to understand, use, and even repair, if they put their mind to it. Contemporary framebuilders are viewed as romantically and glamorously as graffiti writers and street artists today: While the high-tech designers chase down potential innovation, framebuilders are celebrating innovations that long ago proved their worth.

The craft of framebuilding has its venerable roots in both Italy and France; ask Dustin Nordhus, owner of Cicli Berlinetta who deals almost solely in Italian frames and parts. The only noticeable departure Nordhus makes from Italian products is for a bespoke Spanish shoemaker and leatherwork cooperative that produces his riding shoes, bags, cases, and saddles. At any rate, whatever the nation, it's the artisanry that counts.

Perhaps one of the most recognizable faces of contemporary classic cycling is Rapha, whose performance roadwear, social clubs, scenic races, and emotional appeal have earned the company an impassioned following. Riders who favor the classics may don a tweed cap or cape to pay homage to the halcyon days of the velocipede. They may participate in retro events like the Rapha-sponsored Gentlemen's Race or Audax, a non-competitive, time-limited long-distance ride based on Italian endurance sports of the late 19th century (and whose riders are called randonneurs, the rules of the game having been codified in 20th-century France). Or, like the staff at Cicli Berlinetta, who limit store hours to "by appointment only" once a year to ride the classic L'Eroica in Tuscany, they go to feel the gravel beneath their wheels, "smell the talcum-scented dust," and share a love for vintage steel road bikes.

In the end, these pilgrimages aren't about role-playing and playacting. They are sophisticated homages to the physical power and creativity of people who like bikes. In the ubiquitous and grown-up cycling culture of our day, bikes are embedded in more lives than ever. There is no need to feel nostalgic for days and values gone by, no need to sigh: ah, they just don't make them like that anymore. Because actually, somewhere not far from where you are right now, they do.

ANJOU VÉLO VINTAGE pages 108–109

CUSTOMIZING BIKE FASHION BOU-TIQUE

FIXED GEAR ACCESSORIES SHOPS

COMMUTER

1

VANGUARD

As Vanguard Bicycles, design team Shaun Quah and Jacinta Sonja Neoh, founders of the multidisciplinary design studio Angelus Novus, have contributed to Singapore's burgeoning bicycle culture with their customization and restoration of classic bikes along with their unique, one-off bicycles. Shaun and Jacinta draw inspiration from art, architecture, music, and the proportions of classic bicycles and motorcycles for their designs, and work with teams in Singapore as well as Portland, Oregon to realize them.

1 YURA 2 DEXTER

2

COFFEE WALL BRANDING #2

1

DOSNOVENTA

Dosnoventa means "290" in Spanish, referring to the bottom bracket height of every bike in their line. Specializing in handmade urban track bikes in carbon, steel, or aluminum, Dosnoventa was founded in 2010 by Juanma Pozo and Juan Guadalajara, the people behind Cream Bikes & Things, a fixed gear shop and mainstay of the fixed gear scene in Barcelona. Dosnoventa frames are built in Italy according to specification and then sent to Barcelona, where the bike is assembled in house. Thanks to their cult following, Dosnoventa now has a team of riders to test their bikes and represent the brand at international events.

1
HOUSTON RAW

DOSNOVENTA

FIX

1

2

DOSNOVENTA

1
BARCELONA

2
HOUSTON LIME

3
TOKYO

4
DETROIT

3

4

MAXXIS.com

MISERICORDIA × ABICI *FUGA*

The only fashion label from Peru of international repute, Misericordia was founded in 2002 by French designer Aurelyen with the aim of creating premium fashion according to sustainable production practices. Misericordia recently partnered with Italian maker of classical bicycles, Abici, to produce a limited edition bicycle series. Sporting the Misericordia signature colors of dark blue and white are the Corsa, an urban racing bike and replica of a 1950s model, the Fuga, an elegant fixie, and the Velocino, a reinterpretation of the Drasienne from the 1930s. Complementing the bike range with gentlemanly verve is Aurelyen especially created line of casually elegant retro-style jackets, t-shirts, and polo shirts.

Opposite page
VANGUARD *GIRES*

PEUGEOT DESIGN LAB *DL121*

OHANA FIXED / VICTATE Taking their name from the Hawaiian word for "family," Ohana Fixed, a young fixed gear crew in London, bring their spirit of community and aesthetics to their endorsement of the Mainline capsule collection of Victate, a UK streetwear brand founded by Edward Li.

VICTATE

BIKEID

"Every bike that leaves our production line is actually a collaboration between us and the new owner of the bike," says Anders Dahlberg, one of four owners of BIKEID in Stockholm. The shop, designed by Studio Hultman Part Vogt, is a crossover between an industrial workshop and a boutique. BIKEID offers men's and women's steel frame bicycles in minimalistic design with features tailored to the urban cyclist. The 2012 models have two gears and a coaster brake built into the hub, in addition to a hand brake. Customers can choose from more than 10,000 color combinations of frame, chains, tires, and fenders, and add components for an individualized design.

COMMUTER

COMMUTER

* ACCESS.
PERSONALISATION.

This page
CANDY CRANKS Online since 2009, candycranks.com presents itself as a forum for "chicks that spin around the globe," offering a view of cycling culture from a decidedly female perspective. Candy Cranks founder and cycling enthusiast Meg Lofts also designs and sells bespoke cycling products, from t-shirts and jewelry to chainrings and framesets under the Candy Cranks brand. The frames and signature Candy Cranks customizable frameset are built by Loft's partner Tarn Mott, of Primate Cycles. Lofts ironically noted that "initially I was designing with females in mind, but as it turns out, we have more male than female customers."

Opposite page
STEVEN NERERO For Rapha's ongoing survey of the "sartorial street cyclist, observed," long-time bicycle lover Steven Nerero was invited to challenge the reputation of Los Angeles as a strictly car-driven society with his photographs of the city's many and diverse cyclists.

BIKEID PERSONALISATION

BIKE BY ME

Bike By Me makes customizing your bicycle as simple as the tap of a trackpad. Offering one bike frame in two sizes, the Swedish bike company allows you to pick your colors of choice for the bicycle's nine major parts through a simple online configurator. Once the configuration and order is complete, your personalized, single speed bicycle is normally completed in two to five days and shipped internationally within about a week.

COMMUTER

SPURCYCLE *GRIPRINGS* Brothers Nick and Clint Slone literally kicked off their California-based bicycle accessory business with the launch of their GripRings, which came to life via a month-long Kickstarter project in 2012. GripRings are customizable in color and length. The 17 mm-wide, silicone rubber rings are sold in pairs and can be added to handlebars according to preference. The rings are fixed at the end of the handlebar with a Spurcycle locking end plug. An online GripRings builder allows customers to individualize their GripRings purchase in color and quantity.

Opposite page

MIXIE BIKE

With a full-sized hybrid frame sporting compact 20" wheels, the Mixie Bike is a mashup of fixed gear philosophy, fashion, and urban lifestyle. The smaller wheels make it a compact companion that is easy to store and transport on commuter trains, and agile enough to maneuver city streets and trick riding. The wide range of upbeat color combinations satisfies diverse conscious tastes.

mixie

mixie

mixie

MOTO BICYCLES *MOTO URBAN PEDAL*
Pedals are where the body transfers its power into the bicycle. While road cycling has optimized their efficiency with clipless pedals, little has been done for everyday, urban cyclists—until now. After four years of development, Berlin-based BMX champion and Moto Bicycles founder Ali Reza Barjesteh has created the Moto Urban Pedal. Made of weatherproofed laminated plywood with a replaceable grip tape surface available in a variety of patterns, the stylish Moto pedal offers a wide surface (92 x 77 mm) for more foot power for all shoe types and bare feet. At 320 g per pair and 15 mm thin, these could be the lightest and flattest platform pedals on the market. Thanks to its patented sandwich construction with embedded spindle, the Moto pedal eliminates the danger of riders being whacked in the shin by a spinning pedal.

BOOKMAN

The Bookman Light is a slim, portable bike light set for the style conscious urban bicyclist. Available in a range of playful colors, the light combines minimalist design with no-nonsense functionality. A large rubber button makes it possible to operate the light with gloves on. An elastic pull makes the light simple to mount and detach from the saddle pole or handlebar. The weatherproof, battery operated lights shine white for the front and red for the back of the bike, and offer three modes: slow flashing, fast flashing, and steady light. The light was designed by Mattis Bernstone and Robin Dafnäs as the first product line for Bookman, a Stockholm-based company that makes accessories for bikes and the urban bicyclist.

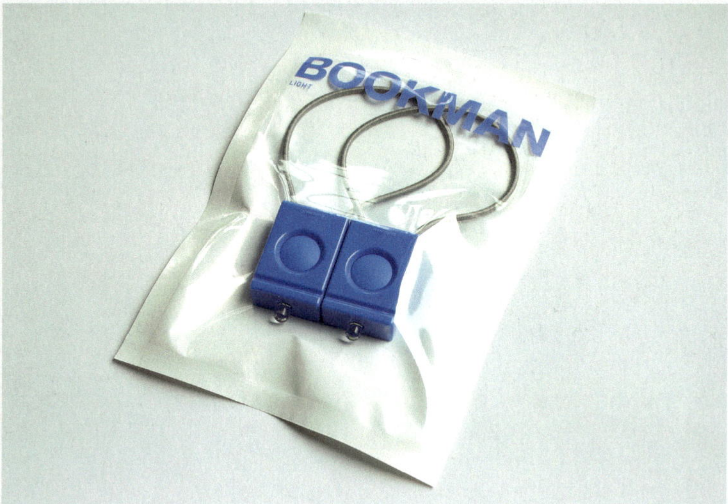

CICLI
STRONGLIGHT
STRONGLIGHT

TINO POHLMANN *VELOCITÁ* One of the main themes in the work of Berlin-based photographer Tino Pohlmann is the world of sports. His commercial work can be seen in campaigns for the likes of Canyon Bicycles, Ergon Bike Ergonomics, and Cicli Berlinetta, to name a few. His 2005 book *Rotation-Contraction-Inspiration* presents emotional black-and-white images taken by Pohlmann of the Tour de France. His newest book *Captured*, published for the centennial of the Tour de France in 2013, is a more comprehensive documentation of his more than 10-year love affair with the race, revealing the Tour de France as a myth that goes beyond the sport.

BROOKS
ENGLAND
BROOKS
ENGLAND
BROOKS
ENGLAND

BROOKS ENGLAND
BICYCLE SADDLES & ACCESSORIES

It began in 1866 with cycle seat patent number 5,135. Birmingham's John Boultbee Brooks had started out in the mid-19th century making horse saddles, but today his bicycle saddles have become an icon of classic design. Leather saddles may be up to three times heavier than modern carbon-fiber or plastic ones, but for some riders, the organic, high-quality look and feel and the enduring, long-distance comfort of a Brooks saddle makes it worth the weight.

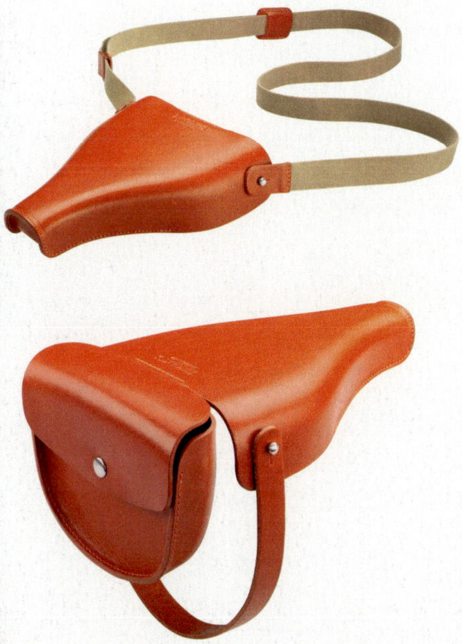

IAN MAHAFFY *VICTORIA SADDLE BAG FOR BROOKS* Created by Copenhagen-based designer Ian Mahaffy for the iconic bicycle saddle manufacturer Brooks England, the Victoria Saddle Bag started off as a saddle cover with integrated saddle bag: "Observing how women carried their bags while cycling and the problems associated, along with the problems of using existing saddle bags in inner city environments, we started to think about how a bag could be more integrated with the bicycle, make for an easier ride, and be easy to add and remove." Brooks recently launched a shoulder strap version of the bag in a range of new colors; while the new version is no longer meant to fit the saddle, it does maintain the bag's iconic saddle shape.

A Brooks saddle comprises a leather piece stretched between a metal cantle plate at the back of the seat and at its nose, which is then battened down with steel or copper rivets. The nose piece is moved, using a threaded bolt, independently of the rails, to carefully tension the leather. Leather, of course, makes for that good old-fashioned and natural type of personalization: With use, the saddle forms itself to its rider, creating "dimples" around the sit bones, as fibers in the hide break down over time and under weight. It is precisely because it takes 1,000 miles or so to break in a Brooks saddle that it is a legacy object, something that a user will never get rid of once it forms to his or her body. (Granted, Brooks leather isn't waterproof, but it does "breathe" away sweat, and water-resistance can be improved by rubbing it with Brooks Proofide, which was once whispered to be made from the fat of hanged men.) →

→ Brooks' company had the innately fashionable qualities of its era. By 1882, it had launched the Climax saddle, a line of bike belts and small trunks, and by 1896, racing saddles, panniers, and carry-alls for motor-bikes—all handsomely presented in hand-illustrated catalogs. By 1910, there were Spring On boots in which to wrap one's trousers, picnic basket set-ups, full-color Arts & Crafts era promotional posters, and even luggage. The modern cut-out saddle has been on the market for 10 years, but Brooks made the first one 110 years ago. Named as if they were jet fighters (a letter followed by a number) the B9, B10, and B11 were the most popular early racing seats and, by now, the B17 has been in production for over a century.

Brooks has always been a forward-looking brand. Today it offers fashion, too: The Elder Street jacket is made from water-repellent tweed and couldn't look more swank even though it counts as performance roadwear and has technical features that include shaped sleeves, an angled storm welt back pocket with entry from below, Ventile elbow patches in contrast fabric for extra protection, and even a reflective Boultbee strap.

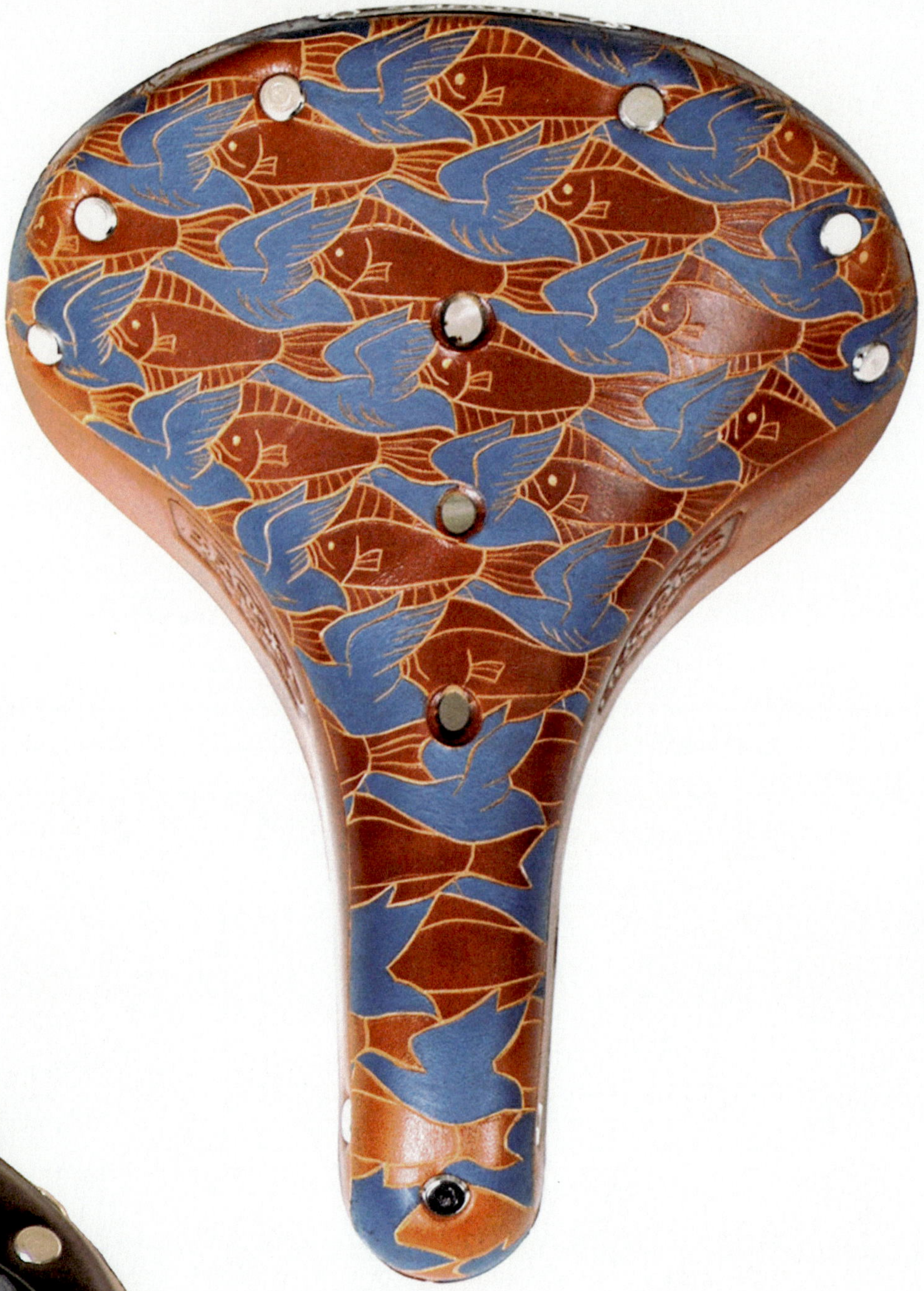

The brand also seeks out artisans and offers one-off and limited-edition saddles. Wisconsin-based leather artisan Kara Ginther hand-carved a popular series for Brooks that included saddles tattooed with various patterns: damask, Japanese erotica, Byzantine elephants and gryphons, Fair Isle sweater patterns and banded tweed, and even a tribute to Escher. By now the company is up to the double spring-loaded city and heavy duty leisure saddle, the B190, and counting. ◇

Previous + Left page
KARA GINTHER *CUSTOMIZED BROOKS SADDLES*

This page
SINT CHRISTOPHORUS Four wheels good, two wheels better? As a car designer, Michiel van den Brink won the Good Design Award of the Chicago Athenaeum for his tribute to Ferrari, the Vandenbrink GTO. But he is also a passionate cyclist, running the St. Christophorus blog dedicated to bicycle traveling in the Benelux. Named after the patron saint of travelers, the blog showcases travelogs, travel bikes, and Van den Brink's own bespoke bicycle creations. His filigree hand-engraved Brooks saddles are functional works of art, gaining a life of their own as form and patina respond to their riders over time. Van den Brink was recently commissioned by Brooks to design saddles for the RetroRonde of Flanders.

1

TOKYOBIKE

A strong believer in the concept of Tokyo Slow—enjoying the ride as much as the destination—Tokyobike is in the process of successfully exporting its fixed gear bikes to the metropolises of the world. Available in a variety of compact steel frames, slender tires, and now a spritely 20" small tire version, Tokyobikes are sleek and stylish, reflecting the city they were born in. The brand was founded in 2002 by Ichiro Kanai and has since opened flagships in Singapore, Melbourne, London, and Berlin. Like the bikes themselves, the boutiques are minimalist yet friendly in design, focused on presenting the bicycles and their many colors. The aesthetic is different from many fixie scenes in North America and Europe: According to Yu Fujiwara, manager of Tokyobike London, Tokyo's fixie culture is less rooted in DIY and vintage than in youth and pop culture. Bridging the gap, Tokyobike celebrated the opening of its London showroom by commissioning six London-based artists to customize one Tokyobike each: A.Four / Lucas Price, Mike Guppy, Alex Daw, Soju Tanaka, Simon Memel, and Tom Pearson.

2

TOKYOBIKE

1
Flagship store Tokyo

2
Flagship store London

3
Customized bike by *SOJU TANAKA*

4
Pop-up store London

5
Flagship store Berlin

3

4

1

2

4

TOKYOBIKE

1
Customized bike by
A.FOUR / LUCAS PRICE

2
Customized bike by
MIKE GUPPY

3
Customized bike by
TOM PEARSON

4
Customized bike by
ALEX DAW

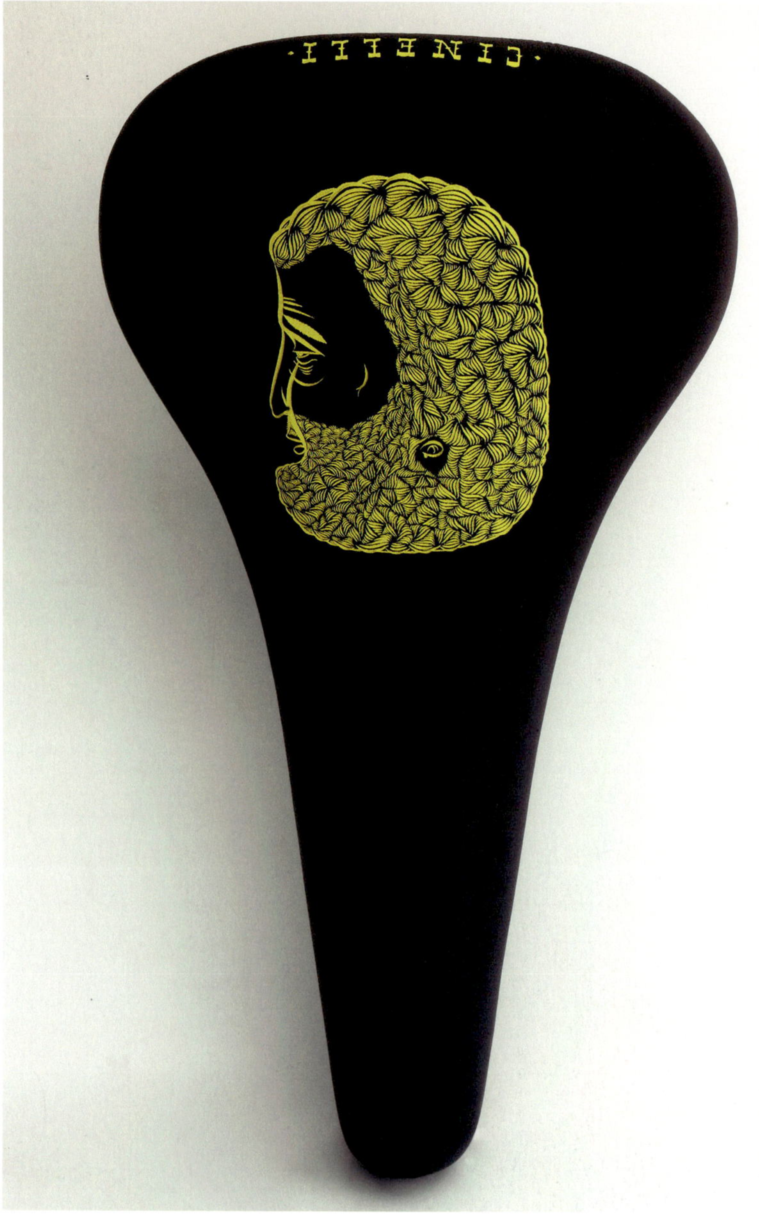

2

1

1
CINELLI / MIKE GIANT Founded in 1948 by former professional road racer Cino Cinelli, and run by Antonio Colombo since 1978, the Milan-based bicycle manufacturer Cinelli has become known as a leader in the design and construction of bicycle components and frames. Since 1980, the company has collaborated with leading designers and artists such as Keith Haring, Paul Smith, Barry McGee, Benny Gold, and recently Mike Giant, a seminal figure in the San Francisco 1990s underground art scene known for his work as a graffiti artist, illustrator, and tattooist. For the past two years, Giant's signature black-and-white graphics have graced Cinelli catalog covers, posters, handlebar tape, and the Cinelli RAM Mike Giant Edition, a limited edition of the first-ever integrated carbon fiber stem and handlebar.

2
CINELLI / BERRY MCGEE
UNICANITOR SADDLE

3
GEEKHOUSE *CX KIT*

3

ULTRACICLI *ULTRABOX*

The Ultrabox pop-up store by Ultracicli, the Milan based bicycle makers of "modern bicycles designed by hand," takes its cue from the My Place project introduced during the 2011 Salone del Mobile by Italian design collective Recession. While Recession's sparse, hand-built presentation container showcased strictly DIY furniture designs, the Ultrabox has content of another nature. Ultracicli's owners Marco Martelli and Marco Donati convinced fashion boutique Zoe to host in its courtyard their plywood construction containing Ultracicli bicycles along with third party accessories and apparel fitting to brand's aura of modern classicism. The Ultrabox has showcased products from Brooks of England and *Monocle* magazine as well as Ultracicli's U handlebars made in collaboration with designer Paul Smith.

Branding
Access.

This page
QUARTERRE *HOOD* Quarterre offers style-savvy bicyclists appropriately stylish indoor bike stands made in England. Founded in 2010 by four bike-loving friends—Daniele Ceccomori, Clive Hartley, Nick Mannion, and Jason Povlotsky—the London design studio was formed in 2010 to create "tools for moving and living." Crafted from folded steel and hand finished with leather, Hood is wall-mounted and holds a single bike securely from its top tube.

Opposite page
MIKILI *KAPPÔ* For Leopold Brötzmann and Sebastian Backhaus, the bicycle is no longer just a means of transportation, but a lifestyle and a fashion accessory. That's why they founded Mikili, creating bicycle "furniture" tailored to the urban cyclist. One example is Kappô. Available in solid walnut, oak, or melamine-coated birch plywood, the stylish and functional bicycle rack doubles as a shelf, perfect for storing a helmet, lock, camera, and magazines.

handmade in germany

Opposite page
MOYNAT *LA MALLE BICYCLETTE* Among the items developed since the 2011 relaunch of Moynat, the French luxury trunk and leather goods company founded in 1849, is La Malle Bicyclette. Designed like Moynat's heritage traveling trunks, the fully equipped leather bicycle trunk comfortably straddles the front wheel of a classic hand-made step-through by Italian bicycle company Abici. The ensemble may be purchased in a variety of colors without customization at the Moynat boutique in Paris for €24,800.

This page
FREITAG *F60 JOAN* Known for their cult messenger bags made out of recycled truck tarpaulins, Swiss company Freitag has always made a point of uniting fashion and utility. They now offer a R.I.P. (Recycled Individual Product) solution targeted especially to female cylists. The model F60 JOAN is a purse that can be fixed to the handlebars for fashionistas on wheels who like to forgo frumpy baskets or awkwardly shouldering handbags while riding. F60 JOAN is part of a new series of sassy handbags named for the high-spirited female characters in the popular retro television series *Madmen*.

WALNUT STUDIOLO

These limited-range leather bags and accessories by Walnut Studiolo, launched by an architect and his wife, marry fashion and function. Geoffrey Franklin, a graduate of the University of Oregon Architecture School and an eighth generation Oregonian, born in the heartland of the resurging American handcrafted bike culture, established Walnut Studiolo in October 2009.

It came about while he was searching for leather accessories that could match the they-don't-make-it-like-this-anymore quality of his custom Renovo with its original wood frame and his father's old Bianchi, which he had grafted onto a Seattle-to-Portland (STP) that he had had powder-coated in classic cream and brown. Unable to find anything that was quite up to snuff, Franklin decided to learn to work leather himself in order to craft what he needed on his own.

Instead of architecture, handworked bicycle accessories keep Franklin busy today and in each product, is plain to see his love of thoughtful design, architectural precision, and the organic beauty of natural materials. Needless to say, these are products that he uses himself.

Franklin's Leather U-Lock Holster was inspired by Brooks saddles and a fruitless search for a stylish and rattle-free way to mount his lock to his bike without using plastic. He product-tested his prototypes during daily bike commutes. His thick, hand-finished, hand-stitched Leather Seat Bag attaches to the bike with a buckle closure while an additional leather tie encircles the seat post. The bag is shut with a "common sense" hardware closure and its contents secured with envelope flaps that fold neatly into the bag. The leather Seat Barrel Bag or Seat Trunk is attached to the bike seat for easy—and classy—portage. No surprise it's so elegant: Franklin was thinking of antique steamer trunks and the miniature barrels clasped to St. Bernard dog collars when he made them. The Bicycle Frame Handle debuted on Kickstarter. It makes it less onerous to carry one's bike by lowering the point of contact on the frame.

A little humor and insight into Northwest bike culture are behind Franklin's Bicycle Can Cage and Six Pack Bicycle Frame Cinch. The cage is a lightweight but rigid soda, juice, or beer can container that hugs its contents snugly. "A flat can of Coke has been called the racing cyclist's 'secret weapon'," says Franklin. "The quick jolt of sugar and caffeine is perfect to get you up the last few hills." The cinch, honored by Architizer as one of the Ten Best Bike-Related Design Innovations of 2011, is a leather strap that secures anything narrow, like a six pack, to the top bike tube. Franklin's products suggest that, in terms of fashion, American bicyclists are more than a peloton of energy-drink swilling sissies and CamelBac canteen-wearing rubes. ◇

1
LEE MYUNG SU DESIGN LAB *SEIL BAG*
The SEIL Bag by South Korean designer Lee Myung Su allows riders to communicate their intentions to those who follow. Using a detachable wireless controller affixed to the handlebar, the rider can activate navigation signals and even emoticons that appear on the backpack's rear-facing LED panel. In addition to left and right, Driving Mode also includes brake, cruise, and emergency. A sensor detects speed and turns on the stop signal automatically. Emoticons can only be shared when the controller is switched to Emotion Mode.

2
BETABRAND *BIKE TO WORK*
Why should cyclists sacrifice fashion for functionality? The Bike to Work collection by San Francisco-based online-only clothing store Betabrand has created a dedicated range of cyclist-friendly jeans and trousers. Based on an original concept by Betabrand founder Chris Lindland, all models feature roll-up cuffs revealing reflectors made from Illuminite® and Scotchlite™, while a V-flap pulls out of the back pocket for added reflectivity. A reinforced gusset crotch protects from the wear and tear of the daily commute. The pants' higher back rise ensures full rear discretion, while their subtle stretchiness provides better mobility. The men's pants come fitted with an easy-access cell phone pocket.

1

2

HÖVDING *THE INVISIBLE BICYCLE HELMET* The Invisible Bicycle Helmet by Swedish designers Anna Haupt and Terese Alstin unites fashion with hi-tech safety. Concealed in a stylish interchangeable collar worn around the neck, the Hövding helmet is a portable air bag made of ultra-strong, rip-proof nylon that inflates around your head like a hood in the case of an accident. Battery-powered sensors programmed according to a patented algorithm constantly monitor the wearer's movements, sending a signal to the tiny helium gas inflator in the back of the collar only upon detection of "abnormal movement" associated with an accident. The helmet is not advised for off-road cycling, tandem bikes, or unicycles, certain extreme hairstyles, or wearers under the age of 15.

JOSÉ CASTRELLON *PRITI BAIKS*
In Panama, the vernacular term "priti" goes beyond surface beauty to denote something possessing ingenious and striking grace. The portraits in the photo series Priti Baiks by Panamanian photographer José Castrellón depict the use of the bicycle as a multifaceted expression of individuality among young Panamanian men. Here, components are clearly more important than the frame, with horns likely being among the most important element of these customized two-wheelers that are often the owners' only means of (private) transportation. The Priti Baiks demonstrate how a lack of resources can lead to incredible creativity, to craft luxuries out of the everyday.

RETRO RACES

CON-

FRAMEBUILDERS

NOIS-

PENNY FARTHING

VINTAGE

SEURS

RANDONNEURS

ntinental
ION ROUG
HURET
POLSKA
POLSKA

EURO SHOP
SPLEND
Retro Ronde
373
gelati
MICHELIN
A.C.U.

RETRORONDE

Since 2007, the RetroRonde celebrates the tradition of Flemish classic cycling that came alive with the creation of the legendary Tour of Flanders (Dutch: Ronde van Vlaanderen) road cycling race in 1913. As its name suggests, the RetroRonde features riders on vintage bikes dating from before 1987 and dressed in corresponding cycling garb. While the proliferation of vintage cycling tricots and casquettes celebrate the hardmen of Classic Cycle racing, the RetroRonde is far from competitive. During their 40 or 70 km tour, participants are encouraged to take in the rolling landscape of the Flemish Ardennes as they make their way along its iconic cobblestoned roads, stopping along the way to refresh with local specialties. In 2013 the event will take on even greater dimensions as the RetroRonde celebrates the Tour of Flanders centennial.

420

LAINATE

1

2

1
DARIO PEGORETTI The venerable legacy of Italian racing frames has a face in Dario Pegoretti. Born in 1956, he began his career as an apprentice to his father-in-law, the legendary framebuilder Luigino Milani. He trained in the workshop in Verono from 1975 to 1983. Pegoretti continued to work at Milani through the 1990s, during which he also worked on contract for other manufacturers. Pegoretti credits the American cycle company Gita for convincing him to produce under his own name. Pegoretti moved to the small town of Caldonazzo in the Dolomites in 1999, where he and his assistants work primarily with steel to make some 600 frames a year. A pioneer in lugless, TIG welded frames, Pegoretti is also known for his unique, hand painted finishes that lend each of his handmade frames an even more individual touch.

2
PEUGEOT CYCLES *LEGEND LR01*

Opposite page
TERRY RICARDO *CHASING RAINBOWS* Reflecting the bold, modernist cycling posters of the 1960s and 1970s, Melbourne-based designer and illustrator Terry Ricardo interpreted a vintage cycling poster for the annual Melbourne Bikefest poster competition. While it was ultimately not among the winners, Ricardo cropped the image and has given it new life as an illustration piece.

SUPER SPORT

PUNCTURE BELT

Allez!
ENDURA
FOR THOSE WHO SUFFER WE RIDE
FINISH 18.06.2008 → → CANNES
START 10.06.2008 GENEVA → →
STAGE 7
STAGE 8
STAGE 1
STAGE 2
LEUKA
PARK

RICHARD LEWISOHN
FIREFLIES STUDIO PORTRAITS
"For those who suffer, we ride" is the motto of the Fireflies, a group of amateur cyclists dedicated to raising funds for Leuka, a charity formed to support research and treatment of leukemia at Hammersmith Hospital, London, renowned as a world leader in treating cancers of the blood. Every year since 2001, some 50 cyclists from the world of film and advertising tackle a grueling eight-day tour through the Alps. The tour covers more than 1,000 km between Lake Geneva and Cannes and is timed so that the cyclists arrive there during the International Advertising Festival. The cyclists' sheer physical effort was captured at 1/500th of a second by photographer Richard Lewisohn during the studio shoot of a fundraising film for Leuka.

CICLI BERLINETTA
DUSTIN NORDHUS

At 13, Canadian Dustin Nordhus used money saved from three years of working a paper route to buy his first road bike. But instead of riding it, he disassembled it, painted it neon yellow and orange, and reassembled it as good as new. A sign of things to come: Nordhus went on to launch classic bike outfitter Cicli Berlinetta.

Back then, as Nordhus was growing up, so was North American amateur cycling. He studied architectural drafting, took up downhill skiing and mountain biking, and worked his way into the Vancouver bike courier community in a Volkswagon GTI before settling into a bike messenger job in Berlin. Just as he was beginning to promote a booming courier scene known as Berlin Massive and collect steel Italian race frames and parts, however, new technologies were changing the face of racing ever faster: "Gone were the down tube shifters, the classic toe-clip cleats, gone were the leather crash caps and woven gloves," he recalls. "But most importantly, gone was the steel." Indeed in 20 years, the EU steel industry had shrunk by 70%. Asian mass production, aluminum frames and TIG welding began to dominate framebuilding (with titanium and carbon soon to follow). For some riders, steel frames became a symbol of obsolescence.

But not for all of them. In the mid-90s, Berlin couriers would ride high-quality, low-maintenance, daredevilishly brakeless steel-frame track bikes off the track and onto the streets and by 2005, Nordhus had enough business to open Cicli Berlinetta. He found a Spanish custom shoemaker and leatherwork cooperative to produce leather riding shoes, bags, cases, and saddles, offered custom pantographed stems, chain rings, cranks and seatposts, and started a low-volume custom frame line for clients who were encouraged to demand in-depth, hands-on involvement in the design process. →

→ Of course, because the craft of steel frame and component building was born and mastered in Italy, the shop carries mostly Italian gear with occasional cameo appearances by the likes of a Swiss Tigra, a Dutch Gazelle, a French Meral or a German Bauer (almost all of which, however, use Italian tube sets, lugs, wheel sets, and parts). Nordhus' products and his team focus on the classic look of vintage race bikes and the joy of riding because, he says, "riding informs our interactions with the world around us."

This means that at a certain time of year all but one poor Cicli employee will be in Chianti, racing in the classic Strada Bianche or L'Eroica, opening the shop by appointment only. Ask what the allure is and Nordhus ticks off a lyrical list: "The feel of the gravel under your wheels, talcum-scented dust, the warming afternoon sun, the wine, the vintage clothing, the vintage bikes—and the feeling of a shared love for steel road bikes." ◇

PISTA
PISTA
CAMPAGNOLO
CAMPAGNOLO

COLNAGO
Bianchi

masi
Prestige
SILVA

Fausto COPPI
COPPI
Fausto COPPI
COPPI
SCHWALBE

Rolls

PISTA
PISTA
111
Cicli Berlinetta
CAMPAGNOLO
CAMPAGNOLO

ERIK SPIEKERMANN

There are passions that are flames and then there are the things that ignite a slower burning love, so close to us every day that we are hardly aware of their value to us. For German typographer Erik Spiekermann, bikes are more the latter: just a normal way to get around the several cities in which he lives and works.

Growing up in Bonn, Spiekermann cycled to school, and later to university in Berlin. He discovered his first racing bike in Palo Alto, and back in Berlin a leisure bike, a Daccordi, which was followed by a Motobecane, a Raleigh, and other German cycles. His collection used to be limited to three vehicles at a time since beyond that, as city bikes are wont to do, they are often stolen or damaged in accidents.

Today Spiekermann stables a variety of types, from an unused electric bike, a light single speed, to a trekking bike or, for foul weather, a Swiss workhorse that features a luggage rack, mudguards, and thick tires. He commutes about 20 km to work in London (on a single speed), Berlin (with seven gears), or San Francisco (with 11 gears) and on weekends, takes a racing bike for more leisurely, though usually longer, rides.

He owns no carbon bikes, only steel, because he appreciates the visible connections that the technology has abandoned. Indeed, he once transformed two old steel frames into simple single speeds for himself and his wife. He has also had two modest bespoke bikes built by Dustin Nordhus at Cicli Berlinetta and Bradley Woehl at American Cyclery in San Francisco. Eschewing the plethora of typography, iconography, branding, and detailing that clutter the tubes of highend bikes today, his are more restrained if not completely unmarked (although he finds it an interesting design problem: on a steel frame, there is little space for graphics and he tends to relish constraints in design).

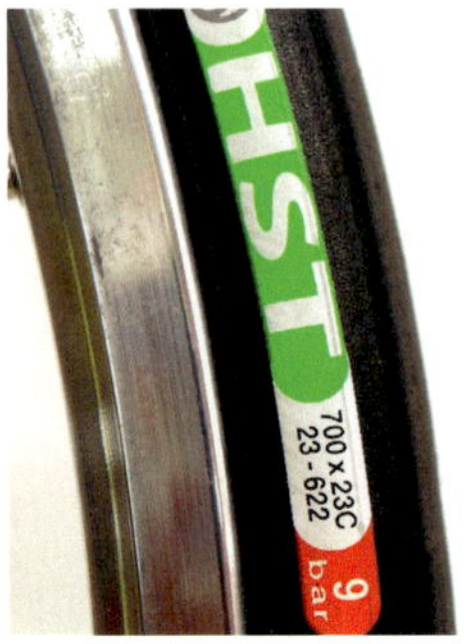

→ So what about a bicycle makes it a beautiful design object in this designer's eyes? It is the most efficient way to turn human effort into movement, Spiekermann says. "There is nothing superfluous about my bikes. I like the simple geometry and the transparent way the up and down of my legs is translated into forward movement."

During the London Typo conference, Spiekermann led a bike tour through the city based on Phil Baines' Typographic Walks. Despite oppressive weather, 35 bicyclists pedaled past typographic inscriptions on myriad buildings from the British Library over Lambeth and Blackfriars Bridge to Smithfields, where they stopped for a hard-earned hot beverage. ◇

PATELLI

3TTT

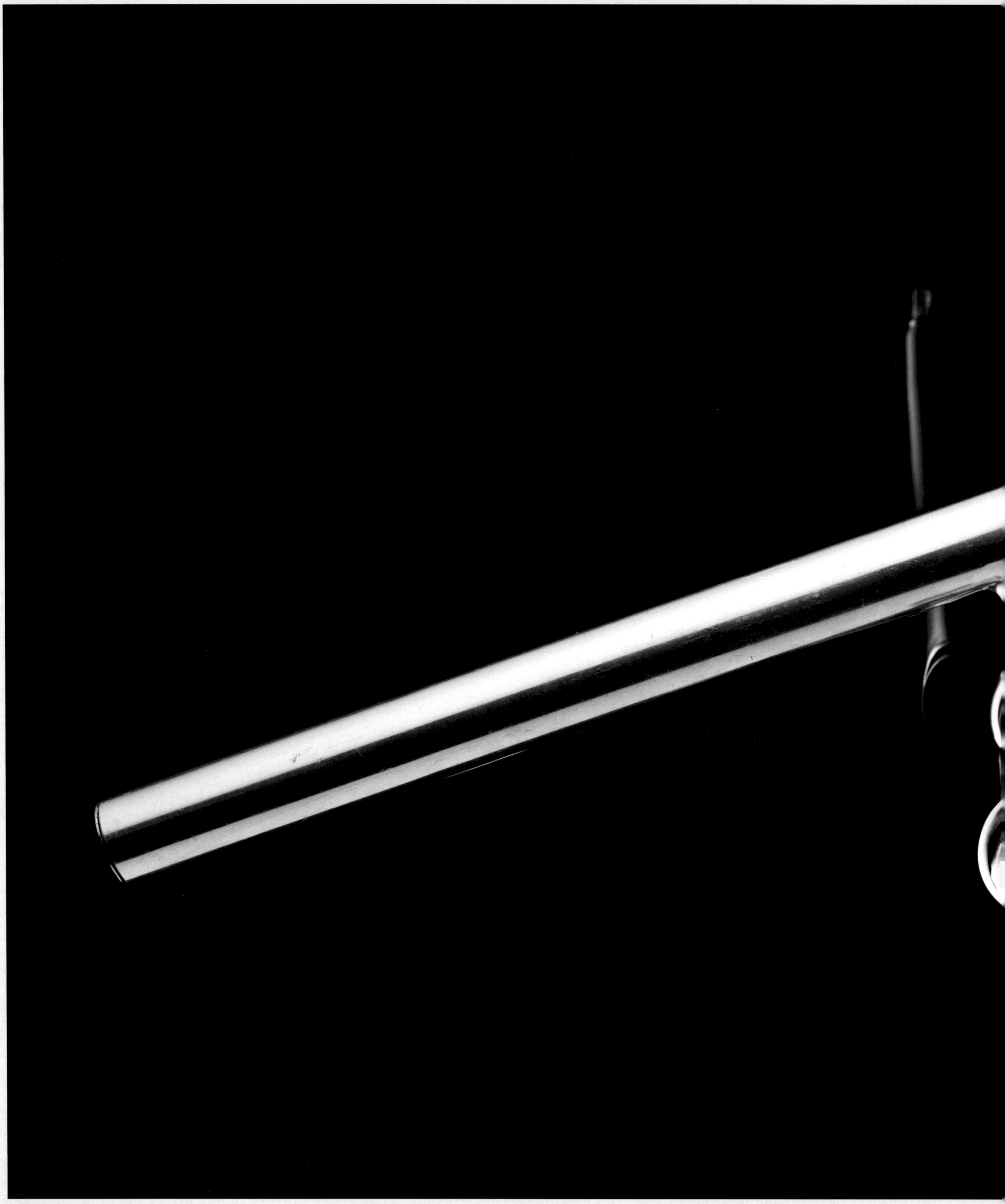

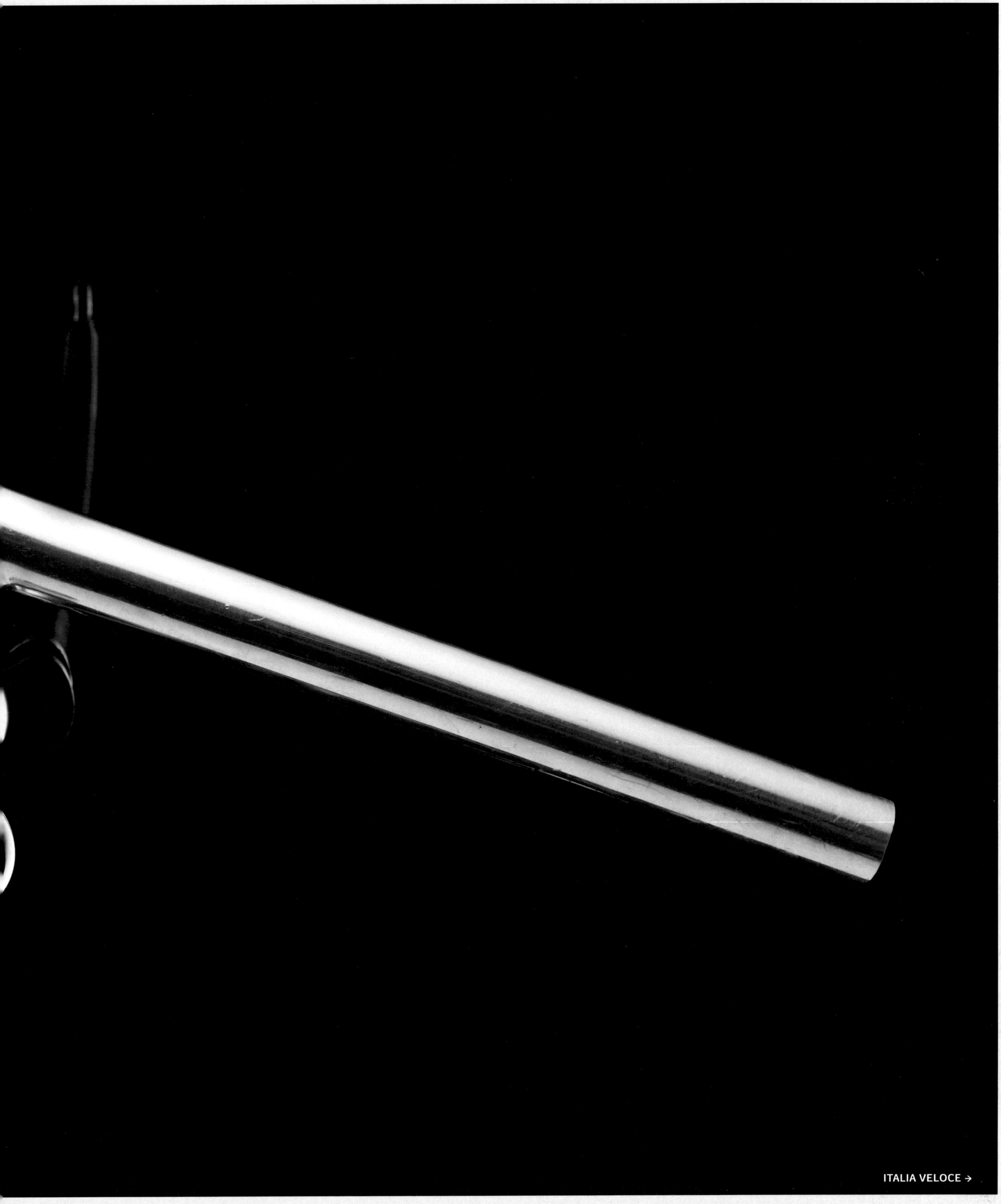

ITALIA VELOCE

The bicycle artisans of Italia Veloce offer hand-crafted luxury with vintage flair from their small bicycle workshop in Parma, Italy. Celebrating the legacy of Italian bicycle craftsmanship and aesthetics, their repertoire includes four hand-made classic steel frames that are customizable with both vintage and state-of-the-art components. Applying a new vision to their passion for tradition, Italia Veloce allows customers to individualize their bicycle with a web-based configurator. Each bicycle is numbered on hand-engraved plates and comes equipped with a booklet detailing its parts. Owners can register on the website to document the life of their bike.

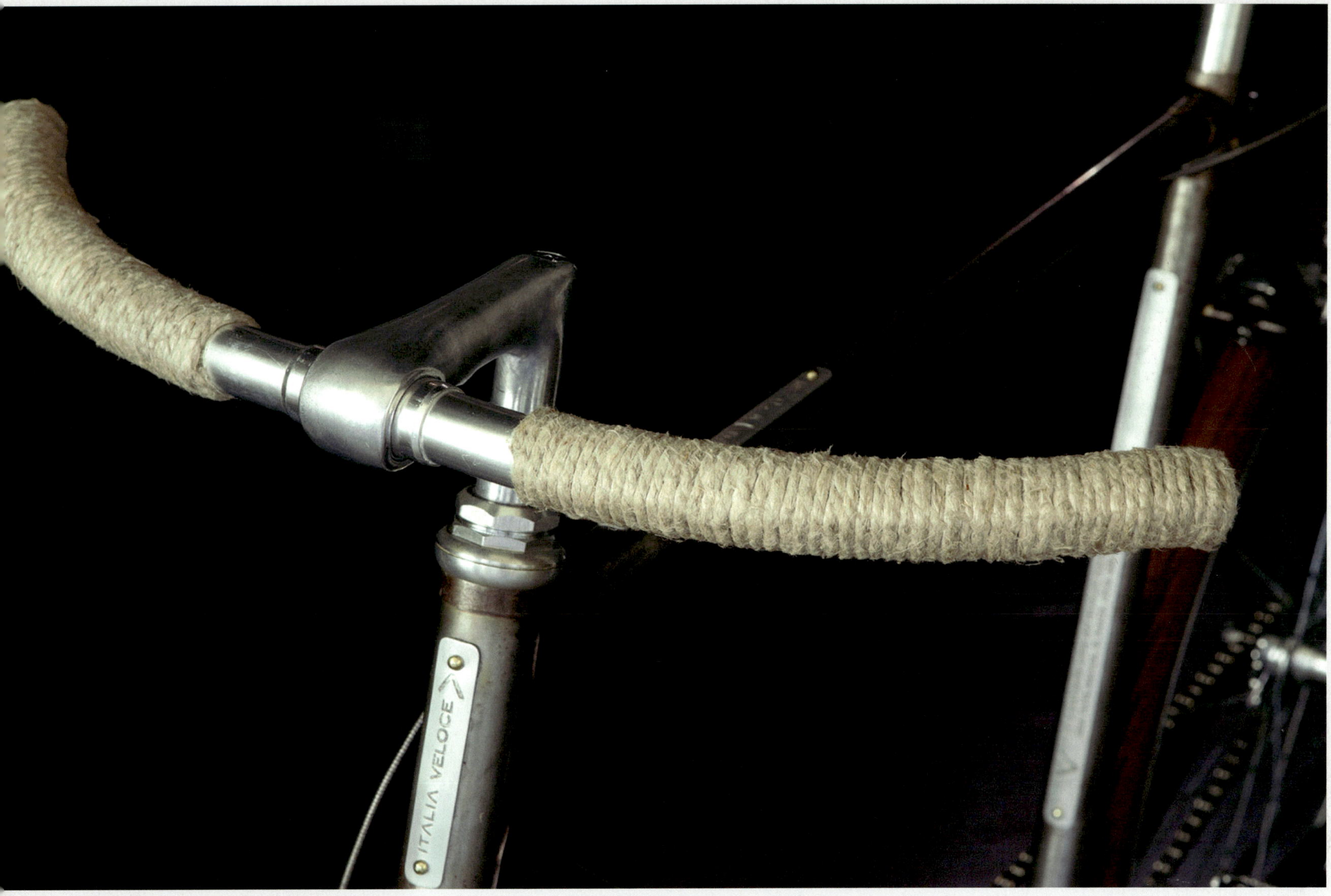
ITALIA VELOCE

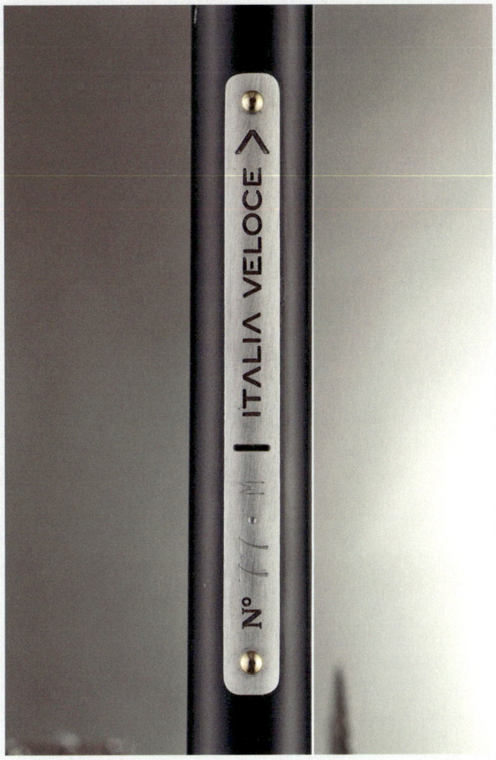
ITALIA VELOCE
N°

KINFOLK The interdisciplinary design studio Kinfolk was founded in 2008 in Tokyo by a group of friends from Sydney (John Beullens), Los Angeles (Ryan Carney), New York (Maceo Eagle, Salah Mason), and Tokyo (Akira Yoshida). After establishing themselves in Tokyo's artsy Nakameguro district as a bicycle shop, design studio, and mecca for urban-savvy cyclists, travelers, and designers, Kinfolk added a new location in New York where they quickly established their talent, their vibe, and their bicycles. Inspired by vintage Keiran racing bikes, the frames for Kinfolk's bespoke track bikes are handmade in Japan by Shiuichi Kusaka, a septuagenarian master bicycle maker. The rest takes place in the multipurpose studio warehouse building in Brooklyn that also houses the popular Kinfolk restaurant and bar.

1

2

3

BIASCAGNE CICLI

Biascagne Cicli describes itself as "two guys and a garage. Or rather a mascot and another who has golden hands with wood." The custom bicycle workshop based in Treviso, Italy is dedicated to the creation of unique, mostly single speed and fixed gear bicycles from used and vintage new-on-stock components. For the past few years, Biascagne Cicli has created one bespoke bicycle per year—in a series aptly named Forgood—whose proceeds are donated 100% to a charity.

1
GREMO

2
ALLEZ!

3
FIXED GEAR FORGOOD 2012
Hand-painted by Riccardo Guasco

1

2

3

4

1
BIASCAGNE CICLI *LA BORIOSA*

2
BIASCAGNE CICLI *FIXED GEAR FORGOOD 2011*

3
GEEKHOUSE *HEATHER'S ROCKCITY*

4
MYOWNBIKE *THE BIKE* As its name suggests, myownbike lets you do just that. The Dusseldorf bike shop opened by Thomas Estenfeld in 2011 makes single speed and fixed gear bikes to order. Myownbike offers a steel frame in two sizes and a host of options that can be easily selected through the nifty online configurator. Customers decide on colors and components in four easy steps, and can check the total price as they go along.

RAPHA CYCLES

Rapha Cycles is as much a fashion brand as it is a performance roadwear outfitter and as much a social and athletic organization as it is a commercial enterprise. In the spring of 2004, Simon Mottram and Luke Scheybeler hung Rapha's shingle in London and today have a second, US headquarters in Portland, Oregon. In short order then, the two have not only established a respected apparel brand, but a hip addition to road racing culture that represents (and dresses) the increasingly grown-up character of global cycling.

MAIN CONCEPT #1

* LOGO – Classic
– Longevity
– Vintage

Rapha roadwear is functional but fashionable, classic but contemporary and it is complemented with items like the special-edition espresso tamper designed by the master maker of cycling components, Chris King, in the style of his renowned headsets, and a range of exclusive clothing and accessories by the British designer and genius of stripes, Paul Smith. The brand now co-owns (with the London bike shop Condor Cycles) the UK-based, black-and-white clad cycling team Rapha Condor-Sharp, owns a majority share in the beloved bike rag, *Rouleur* magazine, and, in 2013, will begin to design apparel for Team Sky, the British cycling team. It also sponsors the Rapha FOCUS cyclo-cross team, hosts events like the Rapha Super Cross, the annual Gentleman's Race, and the Rapha Continental Asia ride, which they then document in short, artfully shot films.

Rapha has established Cycle Clubs in London, San Francisco, and Osaka as social hubs for road riders from near and far. At the clubs, the brand stocks a retail space, mans a café that crows about its freshly ground coffee, screens live races, and mounts exhibitions. They have dispersed caravans, stocked with much the same, to wheel their way around Europe and North America.

With its forward-looking branding, which offers experience and emotion instead of products and logos, the business has made itself a stylish part of a much larger cultural story, a story built from the stories of myriad riders about life on and off the road. The instincts were good from the beginning: Co-founder Luke Scheybeler was a brand and digital designer before starting Rapha and has now gone on to start an iPad-based pro-bicycling photo magazine called *The Collarbone*. Rapha continues to understand that biking is no longer simply a lifestyle, and certainly no longer a niche lifestyle, but a style that fits into lives of many stripes, terrains, and tribes—and it is clearly in the midst of creating what will (not much) later be considered the classics of our time. ◇

giro d'italia

RAPHA PERFOR
THE GIRO
Londres

MARINONI

F&Y

F&Y *LES CLASSIQUES*

F&Y stands for Frédérique Beaubien & Yannic Ryan, a design and woodworking team based in Montreal. Their line of handmade bicycle handlebars, Les Classiques, is the "result of a passion for woodwork and bike rides." Available straight or curved, the meticulously crafted handlebars are made in five sorts of wood—walnut, cherry, ash, wenge, and morado—finished with a natural oil sealer. The aluminum inset and brass rivets provide strength and durability and contribute to their aura of timeless elegance.

LASERCUT STUDIO *LASER ENGRAVED BARS* A simple wooden bar is transformed into a product of utility as well as beauty. Adding a modern twist to classic designs is a theme that can be seen throughout the works of Adam Rowe, which range from furniture to jewelry. The London native recently opened Laser Cut Studio in Helsinki, bringing together a keen sense of aesthetics with digital craftsmanship technologies.

NONUSUAL *GROPES*

The customizable leather handlebar grips known as Gropes are as easy to fit as tying a shoelace, according to their makers, Akira Chatani and Ryo Yamada of London-based design studio Nonusual. Still, owners should plan a bit of time when first "groping"—anywhere from 10 minutes to 2 hours, depending on the size and style of the handlebars and one's skill. The Gropes kit comes with two pre-cut, pre-punched strips of high-quality, vegetable-tanned Italian cowhide with heavy-duty double-sided tape on the reverse, along with a pair of extra long laces and bar end-plugs made from natural cork. Gropes are available in two sizes and several color combinations.

TRUE UNIQUE
THE WOODEN 2-TRACK

True Unique's take on bicycles is to combine the old with the new for a truly unique bike. Founded by Brian Povak and Manuel Dulz in 2009, the combined workshop, store, and gallery is nestled in Berlin's hip expat neighborhood Neukölln. True Unique invites customers to bring in their old bike frame—best something with sentimental value—which the bike builders will then transform into a work of rolling art, using both vintage parts as well as innovative tech solutions, such as electricity routed to the handlebars to power embedded front lights, an iPhone charger, or a back light activated when pressure is applied to the saddle. One of True Unique's trademarks is a curved seat post that allows the saddle to be moved back for maximum leg space.

PAT
PEND

SHAPE FIELD OFFICE
SHAPE FIELD BIKE

San Francisco-based product and graphic design studio consisting of Karson and Mary Shadley teamed up with Nicholas Riddle, a framebuilder and founder of the Urban Mobility Lab at California College of the Arts. At the heart of the custom built porteur is the lugged Columbus SL frame that Riddle based on the geometry of Karson Shadley's own 1978 Cinelli Supercorsa. The removable rack can hold up to 36 kg.

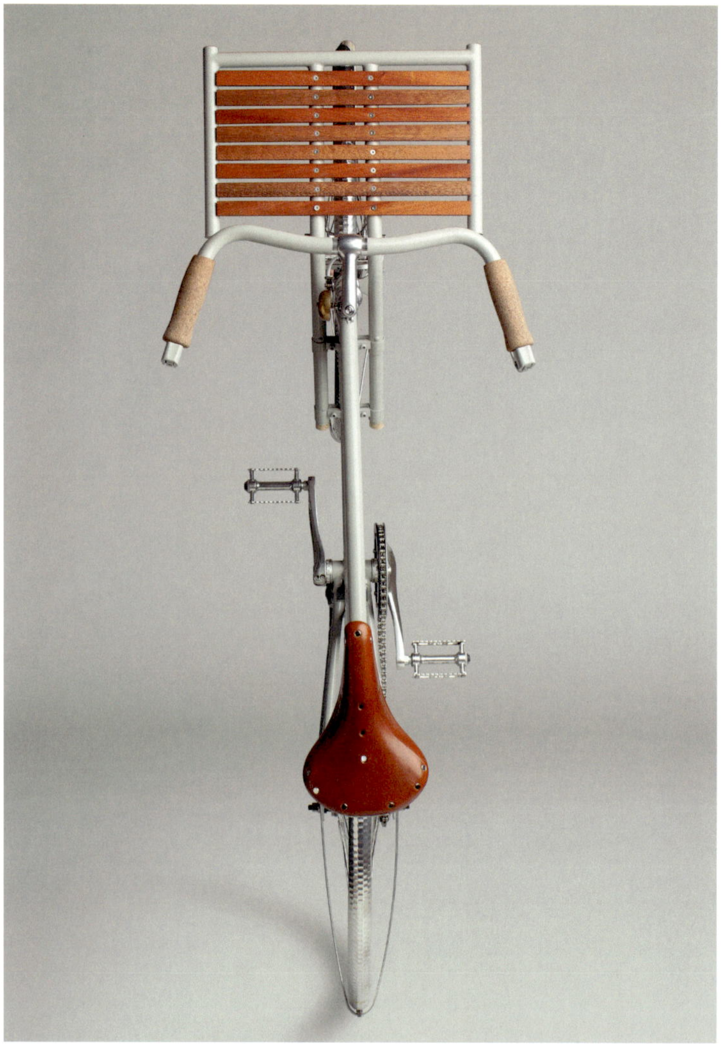

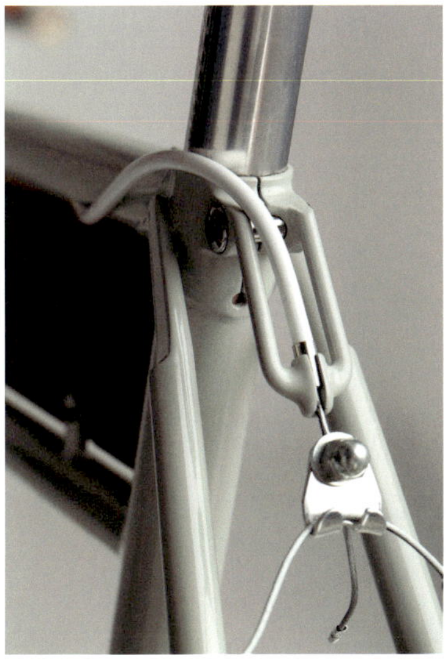

SHAPE FIELD OFFICE

1

2

3

1
IRA RYAN CYCLES *CITY/PORTEUR*
Since 2005, Ira Ryan has brought together his long experience as a cyclist, bike messenger, and bike mechanic to create primarily lugged steel frames made for road racing, cyclocross, mountain biking, and touring. Ryan's handmade bicycles are known for their classic understatement balanced with modern components and performance handling. There is currently a waiting list of around two years for an Ira Ryan cycle. Together with fellow Portland framebuilder Tony Pereira, who like Ryan also rides for the Rapha Continental endurance squad, Ryan created the "Continental," a limited edition road bike commissioned by Rapha.

2
SIZEMORE BICYCLE *OMC (FOR OREGON MANIFEST 2011)* According to framebuilder Taylor Sizemore, "You ride one of my bikes because you understand what it's like to see curb and want to jump it, see a puddle and splash it, or see a corner and want to round it." Growing up with BMX and skating, Sizemore credits an interview with Sasha White from Vanilla Bikes in Portland with inspiring him to build bicycles for a living. In 2006 he took a two-week framebuilding course at the legendary UBI in Oregon, and in 2008 launched Sizemore Bicycles. Sizemore is currently based in Seattle, with a steadily growing reputation especially for his bespoke single speed commuter bikes that reveal simple, clean lines and hand-painted lettering.

3
PELAGO *PIETARI* Located in the heart of Helsinki, Pelago is a boutique bike shop and brand dedicated to creating classic bicycles "that still ride in 2050." Taking its name from Finland's archipelago landscape, Pelago adheres to traditional values of simplicity, durability, and practicality. It offers a well-sorted selection of parts, accessories, and apparel complementing the Pelago bicycle range. Founded in 2009 by Mikko and Timo Hyppönen, the brand started with a line of utility bicycles, and has since expanded its offering to include a number of touring and city bikes for everyday use at mid-range prices.

COMMUTER
GLOUS ROAD
INNIT!
X

1

2

Opposite page
HARRY ZERNIKE Capturing the many facets of New York's "rotating disco ball of cycling" for the Rapha Cyclist Street Fashion Survey is Harry Zernike, who is also the founder and editor of 9W | A Journal of Cycling Photography, and it's online counterpart, 9wmag.com.

1
VANGUARD *BITZER*

2
VANGUARD *ALEXANDRIA*

HUFNAGEL CYCLES
JORDAN HUFNAGEL

Portland, Oregon framebuilder Jordan Hufnagel is as good a storyteller as he is a craftsman. Watching the romantic aura around contemporary bike-making brighten considerably in recent years, he will tell you, tongue-in-cheek, that he grew up in the cornfields of Indiana "building bikes from twigs, corn husks, and paraffin wax." So it is telling that when Hufnagel talks about bikes, he also talks about how much of his life is not about bikes.

He loves cruising around, he says, but he also likes walking: "It's not a priority for me to pedal every day." Granted, he lives near the shop, but he's only owned a car for one year out of the past 12, so pedaling is a lot like, say, breathing for him. He also sponsors a cyclocross team dressed in racewear created by an MTV graphic designer. So, if "passionate" is too earnest a word for his feelings about bicycles, then Hufnagel is, at least, pretty stoked about them.

He did, indeed, grow up learning his trade: in his dad's garage, doing BMX, road and cyclocross racing, in the bike shop he worked at as a teenager, during a framebuilding course at the United Bicycle Institute, and once he had acquired his own tooling, on the job. Since then, from Portland, which was named one of the bike-friendliest cities around and where biking has increased over 250% since 2000, he has seen a precipitous rise in framebuilding around the world. This is due, in part, to the proliferation of schools and access to the internet: the information needed to learn how to construct frames is more available than it ever has been before. For decades, there have been the framebuilders who endured the vicissitudes of the market—mid-century masters like René Herse and Alex Singer who had to make their own components or more recent inspirations like JP Weigle, Peter Johnson, Mark DiNucci and Tom Ritchey—but they have been joined by a huge influx of new generation builders who are scattered not just around the US but across the globe. Organizations have even grown up to encourage this growth: Oregon Manifest Constructor's Design-Build Challenge fosters creative collaborations that reach outside the bike realm, per se, to include stars of industrial design like IDEO and fuse-project and media sponsors like pioneer product design blog Core77.

So, today, while the lives of many ordinary people become more and more about bikes, it seems fair that Hufnagel's life is about more than just bikes. He and shop mate James Crowe will take an indefinite hiatus from the workbench to ride their self-built motorcycles around South America, documenting the ride in photos and stories on wearewestamerica.com. "We wanted to create an outlet," Hufnagel explains, "through which we can make whatever we want and allow it to evolve with us." Which sounds a lot like today's bike culture in a nutshell. ◇

Commuter

LA PATRIMOINE La Patrimoine celebrates the spirit of vintage cycling. Started by a group of French cyclists which is very fund of old bikes, La Patrimoine convenes on a Sunday in mid-September in the small village of Favières-en-Brie, located some 40 km from Paris. Bikes must be from between 1900 and 1990, have two brakes and no assisted pedaling; participants should wear attire from the same era as their bike. After a day of riding either a short (35 km) or long tour (65- to 80 km) through the countryside, everyone gathers for a nostalgic fete, where judges give prizes based on a host of merry criteria such as best attire and best bike.

ANJOU VÉLO VINTAGE

A bicycle event celebrating the spirit of yesteryear takes place in the heart of Saumur in the Loire region of France every summer. The Anjou Vélo Vintage is a two-day event bringing together international randonneuring fans for a variety of 30 to 100 km tours through the bucolic wine country, with plenty of stops for refreshments and sightseeing along the way. Bicycles and dress code should be elegant and vintage 1950s, 1960s and 1970s—this means handlebar moustaches, wool jerseys, berets, pants, and suspenders for men, and vintage dresses, hats, scarves, and handbags for women. A 2000 m² vintage village is set up especially for the event, including a flea market, swing and accordion music, and a vintage bike exhibition. An "elegance competition" rewards the best outfits and bikes.

REYNOLDS
RALEIGH

1

2

3

1
VANGUARD
CHURCHILL

2
MISERICORDIA × ABICI
VELOCINO

3
VANGUARD
BRIE

THE BALTIC BICYCLE COMPANY / ERENPREISS *GRETA* The legacy of Latvian classic bicycle culture lies partly in the creations of Gustavs Erenpreiss, whose bicycle factory, founded in 1927, soon became the largest in Latvia, supplying bikes throughout the Baltic region. In 1941, Erenpreiss lost his business to the Soviets. Over 50 years later, his great great nephew, Toms Erenpreiss, restored his first vintage Erenpreiss bike and went on to found the Latvian Vintage Bicycle Club and organize Latvia's first ever Tweed Run. Now he has revived the Erenpreiss bicycle company with four classic bike models that uphold Gustavs' reputation for quality while adding a modern twist. Erenpreiss bikes are distributed in the UK by the Baltic Bicycle Company in London, which plans to add further northern European classic bikes to its repertoire.

Rubena

1

2

3

VANGUARD

1
CHARLOTTE
2
HEIDI
3
GABRIELA

FOLK ENGINEERED *SUNSHINE*

Folk Engineered specializes in practical bikes for the mid-Atlantic region of the United States, a "habitat of beaches, suburbs, mountains, and urban jungles." Brought together by their passion for bicycles and building them, Ryan and Marie Reedell founded the company in 2009. Starting off with one-off handmade bicycles, they soon expanded to design bicycles for production, providing more affordable standardized frames with customizable options. The couple manufactures their cromoly and steel bikes at their factory warehouse in Newark in their spare time: they both have day jobs teaching building techniques and science to middle school and high school students.

TSUNEHIRO CYCLES *GROCERY GETTER*
Rob Tsunehiro gave up his job as a mechanical engineer for the American aerospace and defense corporation Boeing to follow his passion in building custom bicycles. "I really wanted to create a profession and career for myself that I could believe in, all the way through," he explained. After launching Tsunehiro Cycles in Portland in 2008, Rob soon established his reputation for high quality, TIG welded frames and a keen eye for detail. His current repertoire consists of bikes made for country roads, cyclocross, roads, and the city, including rack solutions tailored to clients' needs.

BICICLETTE ROSSIGNOLI

Established in Milan in 1900, Rossignoli bicycles have been a mainstay of Milan's bicycle culture for nearly five generations. With a respect for quality as well as tradition, the legendary bike manufacturer offers a range of handmade bicycles for city riders of all levels, in styles ranging from classic to contemporary. The Rossignoli shop, which not only makes and sells bikes, but also repairs and rents them, is a landmark in itself, occupying Corso Garibaldi 71 since 1926.

SIGNOLI

MEETING POINTS

URBAN

CARGO

SPEED-

CITY BIKES

STERS

PAPER GIRLS

Commuter
SCHWINN

Falafel + salad £5
Ciabatta + salad £5
Bagel + salad £5
Fillings - cheddar
- feta
- mozarella
- haloumi
- tomato
- artichoke
- sun-dried tomato
- pesto
· porridge £3·50
· muesli, fruit, yoghurt + honey £4
· scrambled egg, toast £4·50
· cheese on toast £3
· Baked potato + salad £5.00
monmouth coffee

LOCK 7 CYCLE CAFÉ →

HACKNEY CAFÉ CRAWL
BROOKS

I ♥ MY BIKE

LOCK 7 CYCLE CAFÉ

Inspired during a trip by the bicycling culture in Copenhagen, Kathryn Burgess and Lee King returned to London to create Lock 7 in 2008, the city's first cycle café. Lock 7's mission is "getting people on bicycles, keeping people on bicycles, having fun with it, and making a difference." Located in Bethnal Green with a view of Regents Canal and passing cyclists, Lock 7 will repair your bike and offer you free WiFi, coffee, and other café fare, while you wait.

Look
mum
no
hands!

LOOK MUM NO HANDS!

One of the it-spots in London's flourishing cycling scene is a bike workshop, café, pub, gallery, and cinema rolled into one. Located on East London's well-cycled Old Street, Look Mum No Hands was created in 2010 by its founders Lewin, Matt, and Sam with the intention of doing what they enjoyed doing most: hanging out, drinking coffee, and watching live cycling sports. Thanks to things like their unpretentious and inclusive atmosphere, spacious premises, large projection screen, free WiFi, quality coffee, and multifaceted beer assortment, LMNH has quickly managed to bring together a diverse cycling public, from road racing enthusiasts, to vintage fixie heads, to those simply attracted to the positive vibe it exudes.

Continental
SportCONTACT

SCHWALBE
DURANO

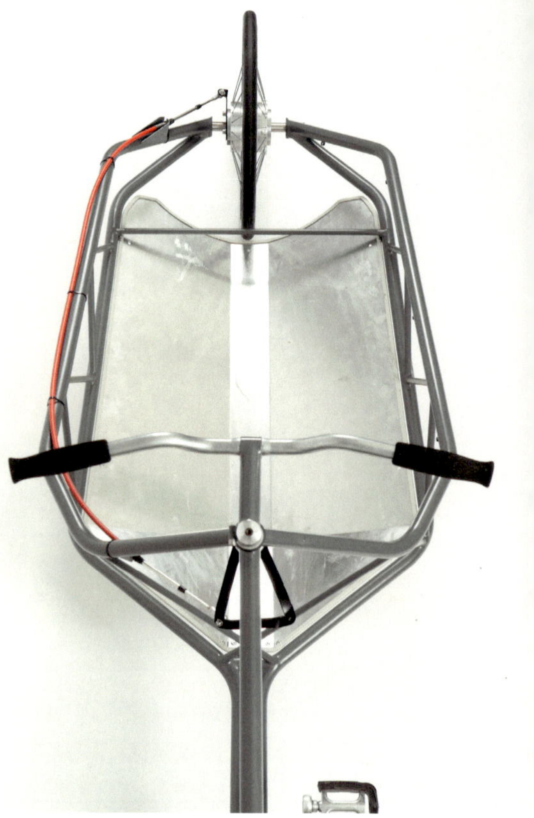

ELIANCYCLES *CARGOBIKE*

"Building bicycles is part of my DNA," declares Dutch bicycle designer Elian Veltman, who grew up tinkering with bicycles in his grandfather's bicycle shop before studying to be an automotive engineer. Veltman has been building custom bicycles in his workshop in the Dutch province of Utrecht since 2005. His recent creation is the elegant Cargobike, a 5-speed, front-end loader with a fillet brazed CrMo steel tubing frame. The use of a steering hub eliminates the need of the usual front fork.

Harry
KOJAK

Harry
KOJAK

YEAL LIVNEH *TWO GO* "These days, we all accept the fact that we should be more environmentally friendly," comments the designer of Two Go, a DIY multipurpose carrier. Using a few simple tools, Livneh repurposed a standard used milk crate into a second bike seat that can also be used as a carrier basket. The design comes with easy-to-follow instructions and brief list of required tools and parts. The Israeli designer works in the field of environmental and social design.

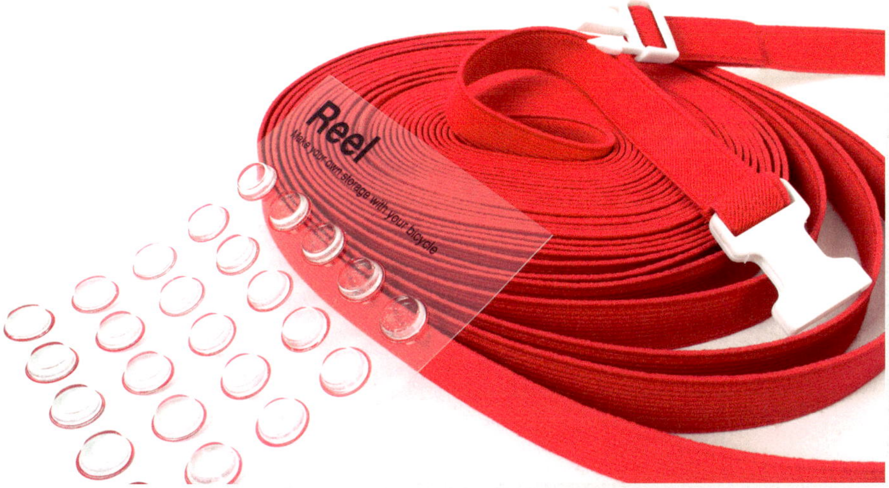

YEONGKEUN JEONG *REEL* South Korean industrial designers Yeongkeun Jeong and Aareum Jeong created a flexible, minimalist solution to bicycle transport. Reel is a long elastic band that allows you to transform the main triangle of the bike frame to store your belongings. Silicone stickers are attached to the frame and the elastic band is wound between them into a triangular, web-like carrier.

PAUL COMPONENT ENGINEERING

Making "nice parts since 1989," Paul Price is a true veteran among the boutique components manufacturers in the US, weathering mergers, buyouts, and economic crises thanks to his solid reputation. While best known for his brakes, cranks, and hubs, Paul Component Engineering also offers utility accessories, for example those dedicated to a beverage that seems to be popular among cyclists from mountain to road: a beer opener doubling as a spring adjuster, a pint glass made of steel, and a flatbed bicycle rack. CNC machined and made of tubular anodized aluminum and hardwood slats, the elegant rack can hold up to 11 kg—enough for a standard, American case of beer.

1

1
FARIS ELMASU *BENT BASKET*
New York-based designer Faris Elmasu drew inspiration from skateboard design for his Bent Basket. Seven layers of walnut wood veneer are pressed together and weatherproofed to create a light but durable bicycle basket, fulfilling both functional and aesthetic needs of the urban cyclist.

2
AHEARNE CYCLES
REAR RACK AND BASKET

2

BROOKLYNESS *UNIVERSAL BIKE*

Presented at the Oregon Manifest 2011, the Universal Bike by New York designer Manuel Saez features a unique frame made from two parallel, continuous loops. The variable frame allows the seat tube and head tube to pivot from 65 to 75 degrees to accommodate diverse rider geometries and ergonomics, while the riding position can be adjusted between relaxed and aggressive.

Public
Work Stand
Hang bike by seat or top tube
Scan for repair help
bikefixtation.com/help
bike
FIXTATION

www.bikefixtation.com
bike
FIXTATION

TICKETS
Make ticket selection
using buttons below
before inserting payment

BIKE FIXTATION

Bicyclists in an after-hour "fix" in Minneapolis, Minnesota can find relief at the Bike Fixtation, a self-serve bicycle repair station and rest stop. The brainchild of Chad DeBaker and Alex Anderson, the first Bike Fixtation was installed in 2011 along the city's crosstown bicycle road, the Midtown Greenway, one of the many examples of the city's ongoing support of bicycling culture. The Fixtation includes a repair stand with attached tools, a self-contained compressed air tire inflator, and a vending machine with refreshments, and spare parts, such as tubes and lights. The Bike Fixtation team sells its station elements together or individually, and can already be found in various configurations in California, Oregon, and Tennessee.

1

2

3

1
WORKCYCLES
FR8 CROSS-FRAME
2
PELAGO *BRISTOL*
3
WORKCYCLES *FR8 NN8D*
4
VELORBIS *ROSA ROYALE*

4

1
VELORBIS *LEIKIER* Velorbis collaborated with Danish designer and blacksmith Lars Leikier to create a unique limited edition bicycle inspired by 1950s motorcycles. Highlights include its patented reinforced steel frame handmade in Denmark, special edition chopper style forks, luxury Velorbis components, and cream balloon tires.

2
CYKELFABRIKKEN / WON HUNDRED
WON HUNDRED BIKE Danish fashion label Won Hundred and Danish bicycle manufacturer Cykelfabrikken came together to create a paradigm of Scandinavian simplicity and functionality in design: the Won Hundred Bike. The customized steel lugged bicycle features a lock bag, a briefcase, and a saddlebag with a stowaway shoulder strap. The limited edition bags and bikes are personalized and made by order.

3
VELORBIS *ARROW* Velorbis specializes in the production and export of handmade classic bikes and retro-style accessories reflecting the tradition of Danish design and chic Copenhagen cycling culture. With an eye to functionality, design, and quality, the brand focuses on upright city roadsters and cargo bikes with "sit up and beg" handlebars, designed in Denmark and built in Germany. Accessories such as leather skirt guards, wicker baskets, or wooden carrier crates complete the nostalgic look. Velorbis has contributed to the propagation of the classic bike trend by offering branded bicycle solutions to businesses around Europe. In cooperation with a green-minded Danish government, Velorbis has established a fleet of dedicated bikes used by politicians traveling to meetings throughout central Copenhagen.

1

2

3

SKEPPSHULT *Z BIKE* Swedish bike manufacturer Skeppshult is a living legacy. Since its founding in Skeppshult, Sweden in 1911, the company has maintained complete autonomy, welding and painting frames, building wheels, and assembling its bikes in its own factory. Today, Skeppshult prides itself on combining modern technology with traditional craftsmanship. Their range focuses on classic upright bikes for comfortable, low-maintenance riding with an eye to good, functional design. Their collaboration with industrial designer Björn Dahlström produced the award winning Z Bike, whose architectural frame, elegant appearance and high-end, worry free components make it a modern design icon for urban cyclers. Skeppshult recently partnered with Swedish cosmetic company FACE Stockholm to create classic step-through bikes available in a palette of six colors.

DT SWISS
SCHWALBE

creme

SCHWALBE

Opposite page
CREME CYCLES *RISTRETTO* (top) +
CAFERACER MEN DOPPIO BLACK (bottom)
At Creme Cycles, "creme" stands for bicycles as a CREative MEans of transport. It also points to how they see their bikes like a good cup of coffee: "To us they are just like Italian espresso—simple, popular, but when each one is made with love and care, it becomes a small work of art." The brand is the brainchild of Szymon Kobylinski, a former rock musician and MTB cyclist who also created NS Bikes, a leader in dirt jump bikes. Creme currently offers a minimalist track bike and three classic models: the unisex Glider, the Dutch-style Holymoly, and the Caferacer, modeled on mid-century commuter bikes. The Vinyl track bikes have high-performance frames by Tange of Japan, while the Classic range features handmade frames from Vietnam; all of the bicycles are then painted and assembled in Poland.

This page
STANRIDGE SPEED *TRADITIONAL LUGGED FRAME*

This page

UGO GATTONI *BICYCLE* Known for his intricate black ink drawings, French artist Ugo Gattoni composed a fabulous ode to cycling inspired by the 2012 London Olympic Games. Originally realized over the course of 723 hours as a five-meter-long drawing, it was downsized into a 19.5×33 cm, ten-panel leporello, simply titled *Bicycle*, by Nobrow Press. The boutique publisher in London specializes in the publication of high quality illustrated books, graphic novels, comics, and children's books showcasing the talents of artists from around the world.

Opposite page

MOTHER NEW YORK While images of New York City abound with countless yellow cabs, Bike NYC and Transportation Alternatives are two of the many voices promoting and fostering cycling in the city. The non-profit organizations got the help of creative agency Mother New York to draw attention to the debate on the new Citi Bike bicycle share program. The guerilla billboard and print ad campaign uses (digitally manipulated) "street labels" that use striking typography to convey an array of concise slogans on cycling culture.

BIKE BUSTLE!

BIKE
like a
NEW
YORKER.

GHOST BIKES

Since 2003, over 500 Ghost Bikes have been installed in more than 180 locations around the world in memory of bicyclists who have been killed or hit on the street by motorists. A bicycle is painted all white and locked to a street sign near the crash site, sometimes accompanied by a small plaque with the victim's name. Ghost Bikes serve as reminders of the tragedy that took place on an otherwise anonymous street corner, and as quiet statements in support of cyclists' right to safe travel. While Ghost Bikes are usually installed anonymously, the first such intervention is credited to Patrick Van Der Tuin, who in 2003 placed a white bike affixed with a "Cyclist Struck Here" sign at the sight of an accident in St. Louis, Missouri, followed by 15 further sites where cyclists had been struck.

BUSHWICK
MOORE ST

This page
CHARRIE'S CAFÉ Rie Sawada loves coffee. And she loves cycling. Her business concept for Berlin, Charrie's Café, combines the two. Shortly after moving to the city from her native Japan, Sawada premiered her "coffee bike" at the VELOBerlin 2011 bike convention. Charrie's Café can often be found on street corners, near bicycle shops, or at bike events around Berlin.

Opposite page
LEAH BUCKAREFF *THE LESEN LOUNGE* Canadian visual artist and musician Leah Buckareff encapsulates the romantic punk spirit of expat Berlin with her Lesen Lounge, a library on wheels that celebrates independent publishing and the medium of zines. "Lesen" means "to read" in German, and the Lesen Lounge offers an itinerant station to peruse a rotating selection of more than 50 zines published by artists from around the world. Buckareff parks her bicycle-drawn library in various locations around Berlin, publishing her itinerary on hand-drawn maps on the Lesen Lounge website.

the
lesen
lounge

BONESHAKER MAGAZINE
JAMES LUCAS & JOHN COE

Boneshaker magazine is an ad-free, not-for-profit, illustrated quarterly magazine about global contemporary bike culture. It takes its name from a pioneering moment in the history of the two-wheeler. During the 1860s, the modern bicycle's forerunner was called a velocipede (fleet foot), except in England and America, where riders had dubbed it the "boneshaker." Because it had such a rigid frame and iron banded wheels, the ride could be a rather tooth-rattling experience. Things improved when later models began to incorporate ball bearings and solid rubber tires.

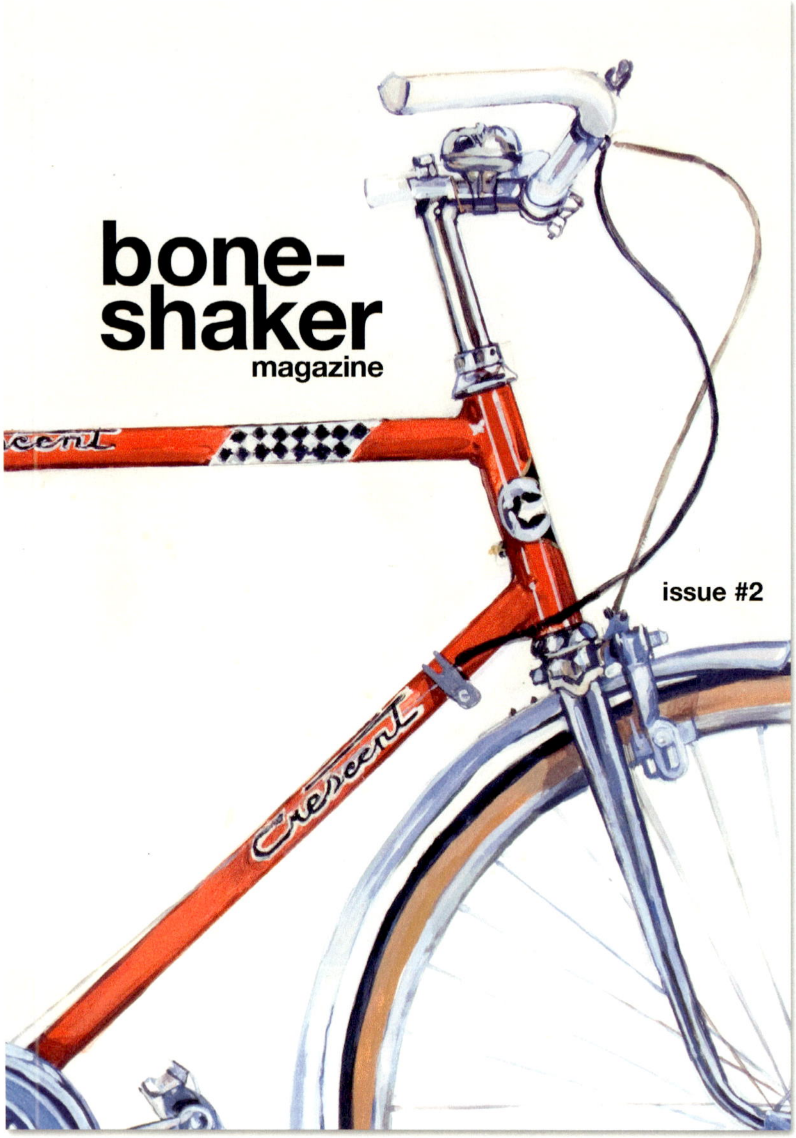

Bicycle Paintings
by Taliah Lempert

Bicycles are so beautiful...

...and such a strong, positive symbol that they still leave me totally inspired, even after fourteen years of making pictures of them.

I started painting pictures of bicycles in 1996. I had just bought a bike on a whim and was blown away by how fast I could get around, how it expanded my sense of self and the city and by the power and beauty of it. I fell in love with cycling and had to shout about it – make some noise. Visual noise.

Bicycles are great; so beautiful and such a strong, positive symbol that still leave me totally inspired, even after fourteen years of making pictures of them. Some of my earliest memories are riding with my sister in my dad's bike trailer. He loves cycling and would take us along while he cruised around the countryside in Upstate New York. He thinks bikes are important and so gave each of us a good 10 speed as a Bat Mitzva gift.

And I love art supplies! Oil paint is the best; lovely, lush and rich, and it smells good and feels good to smush around. I love how it looks, but it's hard to use all of the time and often I'll use other materials if it is too hot in the studio or if I don't have a lot of time. I like being fast and loose with materials. Whenever I return to oil, though, it's like a homecoming.

The bicycle always speaks for itself. I like to look at it and muse. I like the way things catch my eye - the curve of the handlebars, worn bar tape, the shape of a seat - the way a bike has become from being ridden. I love the wear, tear and age, suggestive of past journeys and that's why I'm more excited about painting used bikes as opposed to new ones. Sometimes it's interesting to know the truth and so I research it. When I've painted pro-racers' bikes, I've read all I can about the cyclist's career and looked at lots of photographs of the bike in action. But I also enjoy the not-knowing. I have no idea who rode some of my favorite bikes but I can just feel it.

18

www.bicyclepaintings.com

Founded in 2009, *Boneshaker*'s retro-modern, perfect-bound look, its graphical savoir faire, and the substantial international content it commissions—"from Bogota to the Big Apple, from Slovakia to the Sudan"—make the magazine stand out from the crowd. The publication is managed by co-founder and editor-at-large James Lucas, co-founder and creative director John Coe, and chief editor Mike White, who select stories that ruminate on the manifold and often unexpected ways that cycling overlaps with the rest of life—from public policy and urban planning to art and philosophy. "No training tips, race diets or adverts," the editors have promised. "We're about freedom, friendship, and adventure."

DOKUMENTA CICLISTA

is a project run by Filip K – Polish cycle-enthusiast and photographer living in the UK. The idea behind the project? Simply to document man and his bicycle by photographing cyclists and their "beautiful machines" against a stark white backdrop in cities across Europe. Boneshaker caught up with Filip for a chat:

BS: Hi Filip, so how did your project come about – what was your primary inspiration?

FK: Well, it's taken me quite a long time to come up with the concept for Dokumenta Ciclista. Ever since I became interested in cycling I'd wanted to bring photography and bicycles together in some form or other. I didn't want to just photograph specific 'scenes' or trends though, the idea was always to be more inclusive than that. Eventually I became more aware of the connection between cyclists and their bikes, I realised that this was what I wanted to try and capture in my photography.

44

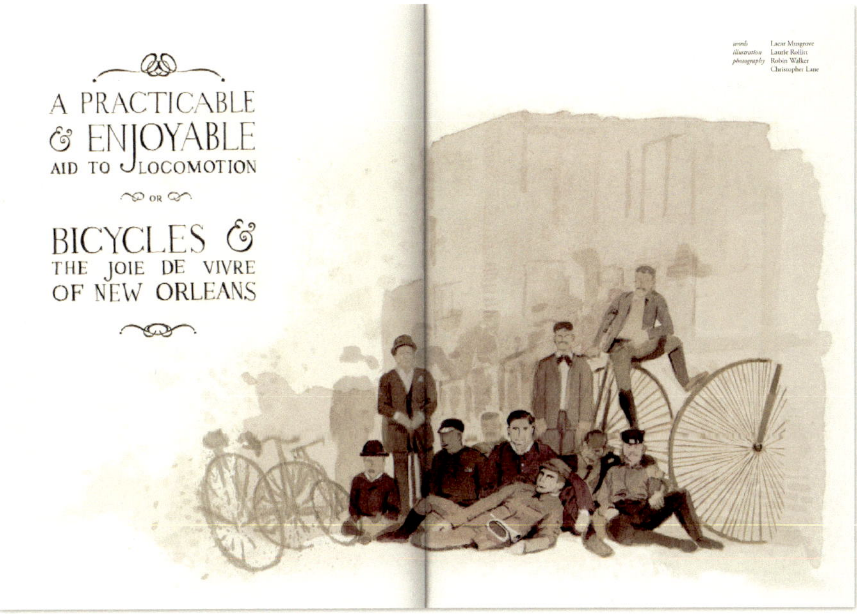

Take Issue 2 which followed long-haul bikers trekking to Lebanon and India and slogging through the jungles of Belize and the snow drifts of Montana. Issue 5 pedaled through India, where motorized transport is colliding head-on with the environment, and then recounted the cycling history of New Orleans, starting from the 1880s. Issue 7 covered freestyle cycling in impoverished Gambia and meditated on "bicycles and Buddhism." Authors Germaine Greer, Philip Larkin, and Jeannette Winterson pondered the sexuality of bikes in Issue 9 while the next number explored the overlap of bicycles and theater, "from dragons to Don Quixote" and the framebuilding artisanry of Londoner Ryan McCaig.

Although *Boneshaker* is about what bicycles can do, not particularly what they look like, each issue is lushly beautiful with every story accompanied by high-quality photography or full-color illustrations. For a magazine so finely illustrated, then, it's funny that *Boneshaker* began as scribbles on the back of a napkin in a Bristol café. Lucas and Coe had already launched the volunteer-run Bristol Bike Project and the zine called *gunfight29*. They had seen the bicycle's capacity to enrich lives. When Issue 1 came off the press, the two men loaded a bike trailer with *Boneshakers* and pedaled around London from bike shop to bookshop. By the time they got on the train home, they had a single copy left. That too was promptly purchased by a fellow passenger. Since then, they say, "it's been tailwinds all the way." ◇

PAPERGIRL

Berlin designer and artist Aisha Ronniger founded the Papergirl art project in 2006 to bring art to the public in new and unusual ways. Inspired by the image of American paperboys, the initiative includes women on bikes who distributed rolled-up artwork to passersby.

The artwork is collected through open calls, exhibited, and then distributed. Papergirl also organizes the Mutant Bike Workshop, where participants are guided in sculpturally recycling old bicycles into works of art.

ROBERT WECHSLER
THE CIRCULAR BIKE

Los-Angeles based sculptural artist Robert Wechsler works with everyday, familiar objects to "perturb the norm in order to demonstrate the malleability of the conventions that often define our everyday experience." His Circular Bike is constructed from nine salvaged bikes, tube steel, and yellow paint. The whimsical yet functional intervention can be easily dismantled and reassembled, making it easy to display in public places to attract a variety of riders.

CYCLO-PHONE The Cyclo-phone is a bicycle-powered music machine, designed by New York-based Venezuelan architects Marcelo Ertorteguy and Sara Valente. Users play music by pedaling a stationary bicycle connected to the instrument, changing rhythms by adjusting their pedaling speed. Made from off-the-shelf materials, the Cyclo-phone consists of a rubber flap attached to a bicycle rim slapping on 8 PVC pipes that are held together in a radial configuration by a plastic stock tank. Each pipe is cut at a different length to produce different tones. The Cyclo-phone was presented as an interactive installation at the 2012 Summer Streets festival sponsored by the New York City Department of Transportation.

ENVIRONMENTAL TRANSPORT ASSOCIATION (ETA) *HORNSTER* The frustration of a road bicyclist being disregarded and potentially injured by inattentive motorists receives an answer in the Hornster. The concept bike features a Airchime KH3A triple air horn, normally used on trains, and is powered by a scuba tank fixed to the cross bar. Hornster was developed to highlight the dangers faced by cyclists on city roads by Yannick Read of the Environmental Transport Association (ETA), an "environmentally friendly" bicycle and car insurance provider in England. While Hornster's bulk and volume—a potentially deafening 178 decibels—is not very practical (and in some countries, illegal) for everyday cycling, as a statement piece, it certainly packs a punch. Read also created a flame-throwing bicycle in response to the same issue.

The Hornster
SCHWALBE
FAT FRANK

VELONOTTE

During VeloNotte, bicyclists gather for a two-wheeled tour through the lamp-lit streets of some of the world's most fascinating cities. The event is the brainchild of Sergei Nikitin, a professor of architectural history based in Moscow. The basis of VeloNotte was the MosKultProg "theater of urban research" that Nikitin founded in 1997, organizing walks around Russian cities. Nikitin organized the first annual VeloNotte tour in Moscow in 2007, and has since exported the idea to St. Petersburg, Rome, London, New York, and Istanbul.

TREKKING BIKES
ON
COUNTRYSIDE FAT TIRES
TOUR
TRAVELING GEAR

MALOJA Taking its name from the Swiss ski resort town of Maloja, the eponymous German company reveals its alpine influences in the designs, patterns, and color palette of its functional and streetwear apparel. Their most recent collection looked a bit further for inspiration, to the Andes. Not only are Bolivian patterns and colors reflected in the collection design; the company also engaged the work of local seamstresses to knit accessories, and a percentage of proceeds from the collection will be donated to a charity project helping street children in Bolivia.

HANEBRINK *X2* Not only is Dan Hanebrink an aerospace engineer, the former national champion cyclist is also the creator of "extreme terrain" bicycles, made to order in Big Bear Lake, California. The project began with the fat-tired Ice Bike Hanebrink created for adventurer Doug Stoup's trip across the South Pole in 2003. Since then, his purely human-propelled bike has evolved into several e-bike models featuring 20" × 8" wide tires to provide traction and stability in tight turns. The wide treads also provide a gentle ride over grass: Hanebrink makes a trailer for carrying golf clubs. With a maximum speed of 40 mph (64 kph) for the X2 and X3, and a whopping 80+ mph (+128 kph) for the X5 Hustler, the e-bikes take riders quickly across dirt, sand, snow, and road, with minimal environmental impact.

JEFF JONES CUSTOM BICYCLES While many would consider suspension a must for tackling rugged terrain, Oregon-based framebuilder Jeff Jones is firmly committed to rigid frames and delivering natural suspension by creating the perfect combination of material, shape of frame, fork, and handlebars, and tire width. His signature 3D SpaceFrame and trussed fork are built to absorb shocks while maintaining control—the fork is also designed to fit wide, 29″ tires. His patented H-bar handlebars allow for a more upright riding position for comfort and control. Jones' waiting list for custom titanium bikes is currently closed; he now offers the same geometry with quicker delivery and at lower prices with stock set configurations in titanium or steel, with his SpaceFrame or a traditional diamond frame, and truss or unicrown fork.

1

BUDNITZ BICYCLES

The latest endeavor of entrepreneur Paul Budnitz (also known as the creator of the art toys brand and store Kidrobot) is his eponymous bicycle company, which crafts handmade titanium and stainless steel urban bikes since 2010. Following the philosophy of "Nothing Added," Budnitz bikes are characterized by minimalist, timeless design that focuses on the best execution of the essential. All of the bikes feature the Budnitz trademark split-tube cantilever frame that is optimized to absorb shock, wider tires, and a carbon belt drive for a smooth and clean ride. Top-of-the-line components are also a must, many of which were developed for cycle racing by boutique fabricators in the USA, Europe, and Japan. Budnitz currently has four models with rumors of a fifth model to come sporting smaller tires for a more agile city ride.

2

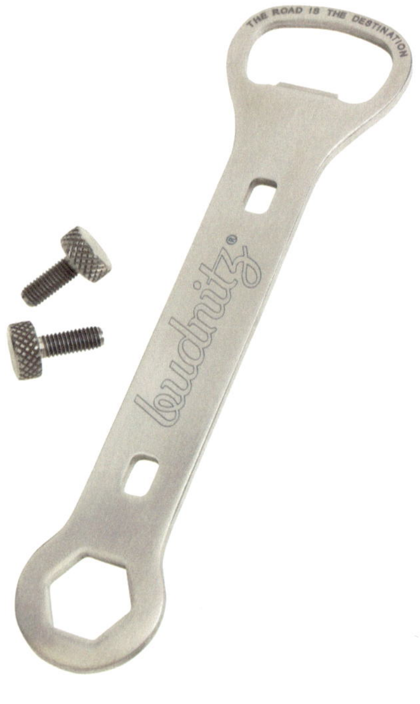

1
NO. 1
TITANIUM
2
TITANIUM
BEER WRENCH
3
NO. 2
TITANIUM
4
NO. 3
HONEY EDITION

3

4

TRISTAN KOPP *MAMALOVA*

When a cycling enthusiast studies industrial design, the result may be like the creations of London-based designer Tristan Kopp. For a 2000 km trip from France to Portugal, Kopp created the side-by-side tandem tricycle Mamalova in collaboration with Gaspard Tiné-Berès. Mamalova averaged 100 km per day with a cruising speed of 20 km/h on flat roads and a maximum speed of 72 km/h.

JORGE MAÑES RUBIO *ULTREIA, THE NOMAD FACTORY*

Ultreia is a project by Spanish artist and designer Jorge Mañes Rubio who transforms the Way of St. James pilgrim route in Spain (El Camino de Santiago) into a 700 km production line. The recent commercialization of the route is challenged by on-site manufacture of alternative objects and performances, through a portable and self-sustainable factory, taking advantage of the specific locations, industries, and people encountered on the route. A rotational molding machine powered by the movement of the bike itself, a tent, and a solar panel allowed the designer to become completely be on the road and accomplish a two-week-long production journey. Some of the many objects produced include baseball caps, plastic replicas of a soccer trophy, star charts, and bio-resin lamps.

KEVIN CUNIFFE

WORLD CYCLE RACING–GRAND TOUR

What would you take—or leave behind—if you were about to race around the world on a bicycle? Passionate long distance cyclist Kevin Cuniffe got a glimpse of the gear packs of participants readying for the start of the World Cycle Racing – Grand Tour. On February 18, nine riders set off from Greenwich Park, England to race unsupported 29,000 km around the world in what has been described as "arguably the longest, toughest, adventure race in the world." Breaking the world record by nearly two weeks, 31-year-old Mike Hall completed his circumnavigation of the globe in 91 days and 18 hours, averaging about 320 km per day (not counting stops for flights, ferries, etc.). Cuniffe's photographs appeared on the cycling culture blog of Always Riding, an online bicycle apparel shop based in London.

1

1
MARTIN WALKER had, left to right, a cheap Bell light, a Garmin Oregon 200, a Cateye Enduro computer, and a SPOT-1 satellite tracker. In the yellow bag is an Alpkit sleeping pad.

2
MIKE HALL's bike has, from top, 2 Cateye Enduro computers, an Apple iPhone and a Garmin Edge 705. An orange SPOT-1 satellite tracker can be seen under the tri-bars. Two waterbottles, only one visible, were attached under the tri-bars.

2

1

1
VALLIE COMPONENTS *SIX PACK RACK* Based in Vancouver, British Columbia in Canada, Lyle Vallie creates custom precision bicycle parts and unique cargo solutions, such as the cedar and stainless steel Six Pack Rack, designed to carry a six-pack of beer cans without the need for tie-downs. The upper rack is removable so that it can be used to transport other goods as well.

2
LEMOLO BAGGAGE *BICYCLE TOOL ROLL* The retro modern Tool Roll by Portland-based Lemolo Baggage is a handy accessory for anyone with a combined sense of practicality and style. Lemolo founder Elias Grey crafts the bag from multiple layers of weather resistant, waxed cotton canvas, vegetable-tanned Latigo leather, and metal accents. The Tool Roll is outfitted with seven hex key pockets and four tool pockets.

2

SWIFT INDUSTRIES "A celebration of culture and an ode to the bicycle itself" is how Seattle-based Martina Brimmer and Jason Goodman describe both the cycling craft scene as well as their cottage company, Swift Industries, which produces lovingly handmade bicycle panniers and accessories.

RAPHAEL CYCLES

"A bicycle should inspire confidence, it should disappear underneath you, be a bomb proof and durable machine of art and quality," asserts Rafi Ajl. Discovering a passion for bicycles as a way of life on the West Coast, the Brooklyn, New York native set up Raphael Cycles in San Francisco's bohemian Mission District in 2009, where he builds custom steel bikes that stand out with their stylized minimalism. In addition to furthering his fine reputation as a skilled framebuilder, Ajl also shares his craft with future generations of bike designers as a teacher at the Urban Mobility Lab at the California College of the Arts.

1

1
GEOFFREY'S FULL DRESS TOURER

2
RAPHAEL'S RANDONEE

3
JOSEY'S DIRT CAMPER

2

3

1

2

1
TSUNEHIRO CYCLES *OREGON MANIFEST MIDTAIL* Tsunehiro took second place in the 2011 Oregon Manifest Constructor's Design Challenge to design and build the ultimate modern utility bike. Realized in collaboration with Portland industrial designer Silas Beebe, the long-tail cargo bike features a leather cockpit with handlebars for a passenger and a reflective coating for added visibility.

AHEARNE CYCLES "Life is simply too short to ride mediocre bicycles," declares bike builder Joseph Ahearne. Ahearne's classic steel bicycles and custom rack solutions are for all types of riding, especially touring, randonneuring, and everyday city cycling in Ahearne's home base in Portland, Oregon. His sturdy Cycle Truck is designed to haul a load while handling like a traditional bicycle. Ahearne offers a wide range of custom options and upgrades, including electric assist pedaling, appealing to customer's diverse tastes and needs.

2
MIXTE TOURING 29ER
3
STAINLESS STEEL ROAD BIKE WITH RACK
4
GIUSEPPE RANDONNEUR

3

1

2

BOXER BICYCLES

A graduate of Oregon's United Bicycle Institute and an avid randonneur, Seattle-based Dan Boxer has been building bicycles since 2005. Combining traditional elements with the best of modern components and finishes, he draws inspiration from the fully integrated classic bicycles produced by the French constructeurs from the 1930s to the 1960s. In addition to full custom bicycles that take up to 12 months to create, he offers the Boxer Brevet Series. In a more streamlined production process, these randonneuring bicycles are composed from a selection of lugged steel frames and forks and one of three component starter kits. Boxer Bicycles include an optional integrated chainrest system that allows simple and clean replacement of the rear wheel without the need for handling the chain.

3

1
BOXER BICYCLES *WJACO11* The Travel Randonneur splits in two with the S&S Machine stainless steel couplers, fitting into an FAA approved suitcase that avoids the oversize baggage fee.

2
BOXER BICYCLES *GYORK10* A top tier Urban Adventure bicycle whose custom chrome-plated racks incorporate housing guides for the shifter cables, so they are not affected by the use of a large handlebar bag.

3
GEEKHOUSE
LAURA'S 650B WOODVILLE

4
LITTLEFORD CUSTOM BICYCLES
PHOTOGRAPHER'S GETAWAY BIKE
Working in the tradition of the mid-century French constructeurs from his one-man workshop in Portland, Jon Littleford designs and builds custom steel framed touring bikes that he outfits with his innovative and reliable racks according to need, "for diversion, excursion, or expedition."

4

1

RIVENDELL BICYCLE WORKS

Rivendell Bicycle Works is a "purveyor of lugged steel bicycle frames, smart parts and accessories, wool clothing, leather saddles, and good advice." The northern Californian company was established in 1994 by Grant Petersen, carrying on the cycling spirit he nurtured during 10 years as marketing director and product manager at Bridgestone Cycle USA. Rivendell presents itself as a philosophy as much as a brand, advocating tradition, comfort, and durability in staunch opposition to a North American bicycle culture embracing high performance, speed, and racing-led fashion. Rivendell works with manufacturers in the US, Japan, and Taiwan to produce its stock frames, and commissions custom frames from Mark Nobilette. Petersen describes his 2012 book *JUST RIDE: A Radically Practical Guide to Riding Your Bike* as a "manual for the Unracer." →

1
ATLANTIS (detail)
2
A. HOMER HILSEN
3
ATLANTIS

2

3

A. HOMER HILSEN
LUDERE QUO VELIS BIROTA PERMITTIT AGRESTIS

ATLANTIS
BY RIVENDELL

SAMUEL
BORNE
RIVENDELL BICYCLE WORKS

the international man's mixte
by Rivendell
YVES GOMEZ

RIVENDELL
ROADEO
BICYCLE WORKS

→ **RIVENDELL** *HEAD TUBE BADGES* While head badges were originally used by manufacturers to distinguish their multiple bike brands and models, by the middle of the 20th century they had developed into a high art. After being exchanged by the industry for cost saving decals, head badges are now experiencing a comeback through the classic bike revival. As Grant Petersen of Rivendell Bicycle Works puts it: "It would be foolish to buy any bike for its badge, or to avoid a good bike because it lacks a badge. But when all the good things collide, a good bike has a good badge."

STEALTH BIKES

PER-

PROTOTYPING

FOR-

MATERIAL

MERS

E-BIKES

X ROAD RACER

SPECIALIZED
DUCATI
TEKTRO
AURIGA

DUCATI
PELAGRO 764
HEGEMANN
SPECIALIZED
OMP
ducatilaibacher.de

PELAGRO Based in Grossbottwar, a region of southern Germany known for its wine and its automotive industries, Peter Laibacher has been creating custom mountain and commuter bikes under an acronym of his name and town—Pelagro—since 2008. His signature frame draws inspiration from Ducati's trellis frame that became a trademark of the motorcycle brand in the 1980s. Another project, the Pelagro Vaillante, "doesn't ride, it glides." The ultra-aero-dynamic bike is named for the hero of Jean Graton's cult French comic series dedicated to the world of motorsports, Michel Vaillante.

Previous page
764

This page
VAILLANTE

Opposite page
YUJI YAMADA *BOONEN* Yuji Yamada is a painter and illustrator who lives and works in Japan. His acrylic and pastel paintings focus on detailed vignettes of athletic pursuits, ranging from cycling to bobsledding. His work has been featured in exhibitions in Tokyo, Cologne, and New York.

QUICK

1

2

PEUGEOT DESIGN LAB

The history of Peugeot can be traced back more than 200 years; the family business from which the current brand emerged was founded in 1810, with its first bicycle built in 1882 by Armand Peugeot. In 1926, the brand separated its bicycle and automobile businesses. Now the two are being reunited through the Peugeot Design Lab. With offices in Paris, Shanghai, and Sao Paulo, the Peugeot Design Lab is a "global brand design studio" applying Peugeot design expertise to the development of cutting edge non-car products for the Peugeot brand and external clients. The Peugeot Design Lab launched in 2012 with a portfolio of projects, including a powerboat, a watch, a jet, and several bicycles, including two concept bicycles and three concept e-bikes.

1 eDL132 2 ONYX

PEUGEOT

ARTEFAKT
SPEEDMAX CF EVO TIME TRIAL BICYCLE

With its stripped bare, rectilinear silhouette, the Speedmax CF Evo time trial bicycle may be an object of great beauty but that isn't really the point. For Germany's online-only Canyon Bicycles, Darmstadt agency Artefakt—known for everything from bathrooms to packaging and gadgets to architecture and one of whose partners is a serious road racer, himself—made a speed machine that the Russian Katusha team rode to a surprise second-place finish during the Giro d'Italia. →

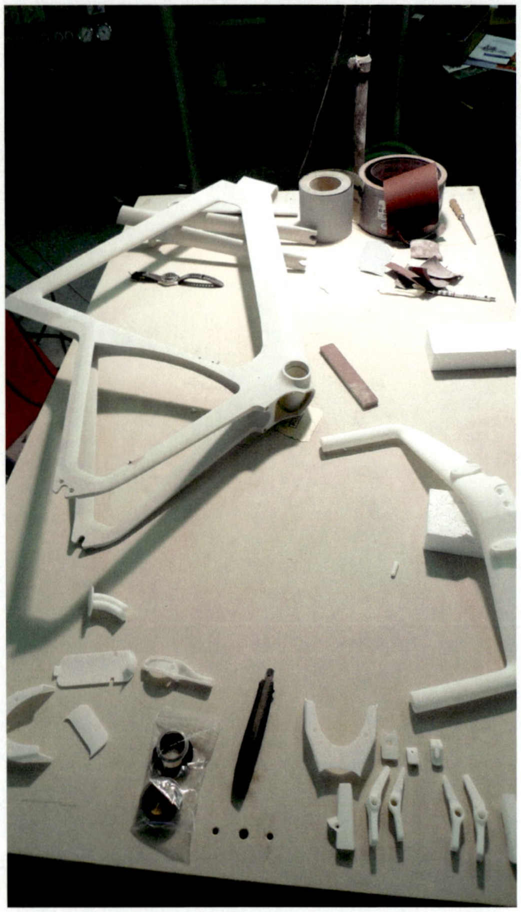
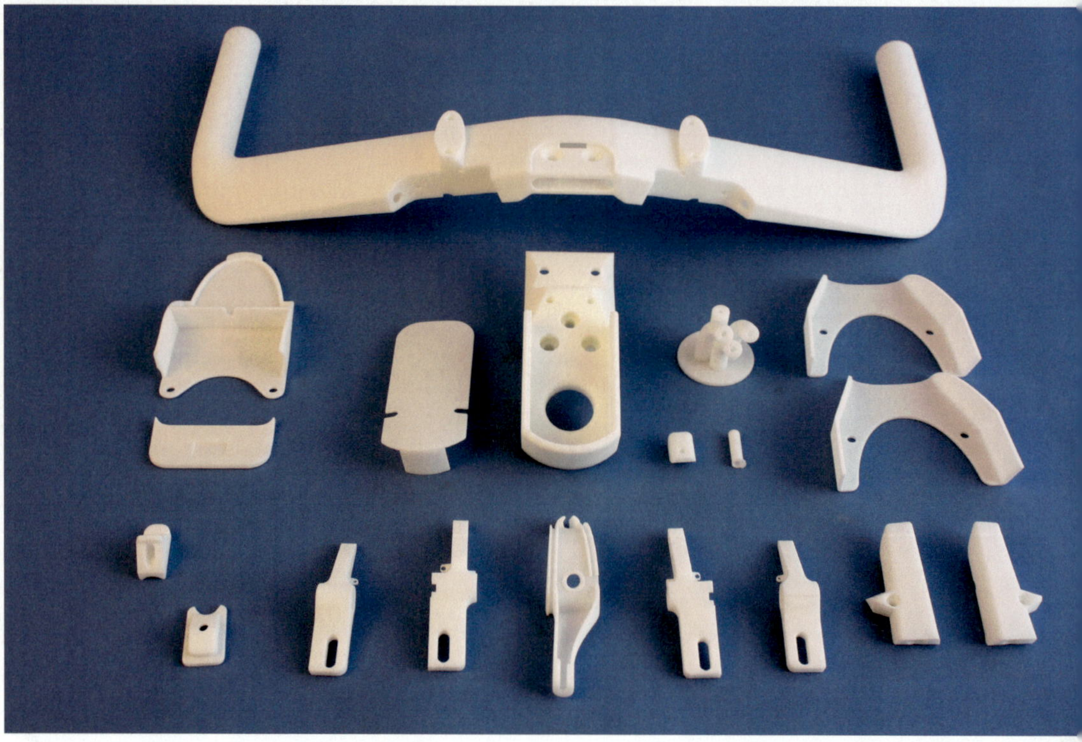

MERCEDES GP PETRONAS
DRAG ZERO

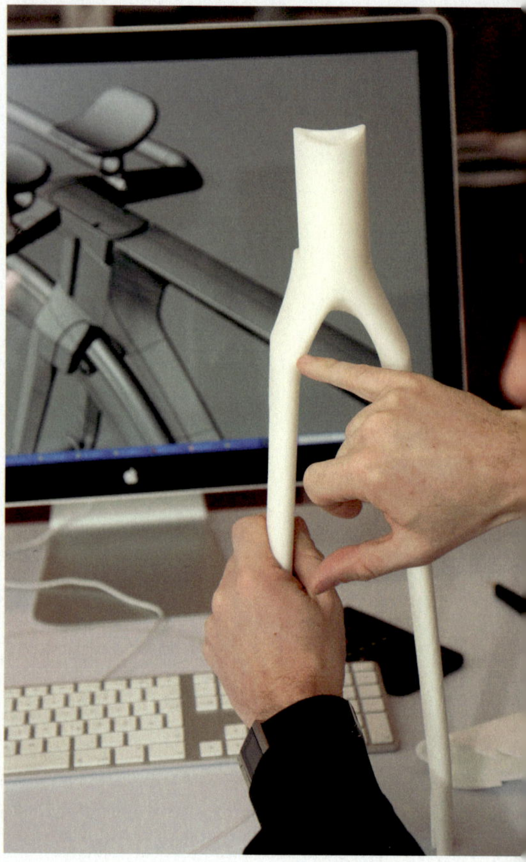

→ Its hardcore streamlining, stability, unprecedented potential for personalization, and materials technology shave crucial milliseconds from crucial races, meaning it didn't yellow shirt the 2012 Red Dot Best of the Best award, the IF Eurobike Award and the German Design Prize 2013 for nothing. According to the Red Dot jury, the design "visualizes its aerodynamics to perfection."

To achieve this perfection, Artefakt—with help from aerodynamics engineers, marquee time trialist Michael Rich and aero specialist Simon Smart—used the highest tech tools around: computational fluid dynamics, a CT scanner, a Mercedes wind tunnel and even a 3D printer to create 1:1 scale models of components. This model helped them to carefully form the handlebars, porch, fork, and brakes into a single unit, for instance, creating a system so integrated that only 12 cm of brake and shift cable are exposed thereby mightily reducing drag. The rear wheel produced in high-grade carbon fiber looks fast even at a standstill and renders it featherweight. Together, these details save riders a lot of wattage.

By using computational fluid dynamics, the team beveled the Evo's frame, giving it drop-shape tubular cross sections and tubes that took their cues from an aerofoil plus some. The new profile, dubbed Trident, of the fork legs, down tube, seat tube, seat post, and seat stays, features voluptuous leading edges that end in blunt angles. This cuts drag for 10% less wind resistance, only a 10% vulnerability to cross winds, and 20% greater rigidity.

In the end, the bike's geometry makes for excellent flexibility and rigidity simultaneously. Riders doing "twisting prologues" or teams of riders doing trials can shift easily into extreme riding positions and benefit from serious individualization (even with a barebones accessories kit). By adjusting the handlebars, stems, and extension type, and tweaking height and width, they can adjust the cockpit into 7,560 configurations (a number almost exactly the same as the bike's top-of-the-line euro value). The development of the CF was the most complex in Canyon's 25-year history and not for naught: bloggers have called it "mind boggling". ◇

CANYON
CANYON
GIRO

CONTINENTAL
GP ATTACK

THE ALPHA BIKE

Setting out to create a bicycle "that would push the boundaries of integrated systems," a team of mechanical engineering students at the University of Pennsylvania created the Alpha Bike. Evan Dvorak, Lucas Hartman, Geoff Johnson, Katie Rohacz, and Katie Savarise worked for a year on their senior project, advised by Professor Jonathan Fiene. The bike features an enclosed belt drive and an electronically controlled clutch allowing the rider to switch between fixed gear and freewheeling configurations. Built into the handlebars is an LCD display that stores cycling statistics on a removable SD card. With the exception of the fork, seat post, saddle, rims, and tires, all parts were made in-house. The result is a bike minimalist in appearance, but high-tech to the core.

BRAŇO MEREŠ
X-9 NIGHTHAWK

From his studio BME Design in Bratislava, Slovakia, Braňo Mereš builds bamboo and carbon bike frames and accessories—in his free time. Mereš also works as an industrial designer and mechanical engineer. One of Mereš's recent experiments is the X-9 Nighthawk. The handmade frame structure was created from honeycomb sandwich panels that he water-jet cut, connected, and then laminated using carbon fiber. For exhibition purposes, Mereš outfitted the prototype with his BME S72 saddle prototype, along with handlebars and a carbon fork he specially designed to fit the frame

UBC *COREN*

Until now, German manufacturer UBC was known among specialists for the carbon parts it makes for the motorsports, aviation, and high-end automotive industries. Now it has caught the attention of a wider audience, as its Coren bicycle series shows the world what can happen when carbon meets bicycle design, no holds barred. Christian Zanzotti created a futuristic urban bicycle handcrafted according to the same standards of engineering, precision, and craftsmanship as a Formula One racecar. The Coren comes in three versions: single speed, pedal-assisted, and fixed gear, and is priced starting at 25,000 euros.

1

2

PODIUM pro SL
MONDRAKER
KENDATIRE.com
EASTON
ROCK SHOX
SRAM

1
BIOMEGA *LDN* Biomega was founded in 1988 by Jens Martin Skibsted and Elias Grove Nielsen with the intention of creating a "paradigm shift in the way bicycles are conceived." The Copenhagen bike brand sees itself as a pioneer in New Luxury, approaching the bicycle as a functional design object for city commuters, which competes directly with cars. While it often collaborates with international artists and product designers, such as Marc Newson, Ross Lovegrove, and Karim Rachid, the company sees its aesthetics as anchored in a Scandinavian design tradition of Organic Minimalism. Biomega embraces a metatech mindset, in which technology no longer drives the design, but "becomes instrumental to the design and subsequently paradigms of which technologies to apply in a given circumstance can be broken."

2
MONDRAKER *PODIUM CARBON PRO SL 29ER* Mondraker launched in 2001 in Alicante with seven bikes catering to the emerging freeride mountain bike scene in Spain. It has since become a leading high-end bike manufacturer with an emphasis on performance and innovation, especially since adding downhill racer and engineer Cesar Rojo to its development team. The new Podium Carbon Pro SL 29er cross-country bike stands out with its minimalist aesthetics and integrated stem design for a stronger front end and high steering precision.

EYETOHAND
THE CONTORTIONIST

The Contortionist is a bicycle that folds to fit completely between its 26-inch wheels. The wheels rotate when the bike is folded so it can be pulled along instead of having to be carried. Dominic Hargreaves' invention is not only compact but also clean, swapping the usual chain drive for an internal hydraulic system that uses oil pumped through tubes in the frame to power the back wheel. The bicycle won the prestigious James Dyson Award for student design projects in 2009, with Mr. Dyson commenting that "its effortless elasticity is mesmerizing." While the Contortionist has remained a prototype, Hargreaves, who has since founded the design studio Eyetohand in London, hints that "elements of innovation within the design are now being developed into production bikes with an undisclosed manufacturer."

PAVÉ CULTURE CYCLISTE

Bicycles are presented like works of art at Pavé Culture Cycliste, a premium cycling shop in Barcelona specializing in road bicycles and cycling apparel. Opened in 2011 by cyclist and bike enthusiast Javier Maya, Pavé makes the most of its 700 square meters without cluttering the space. There is also a small service workshop, a space for reading, drinking coffee, and watching races on TV, and even showers for freshening-up after training. Complementing the cool concrete floor is a cobblestoned entry, referencing the setts paving along classical cycle racing routes in northwestern Europe, such as Paris-Roubaix and the Tour of Flanders.

MAIN CONCEPT

cervélo
cervélo

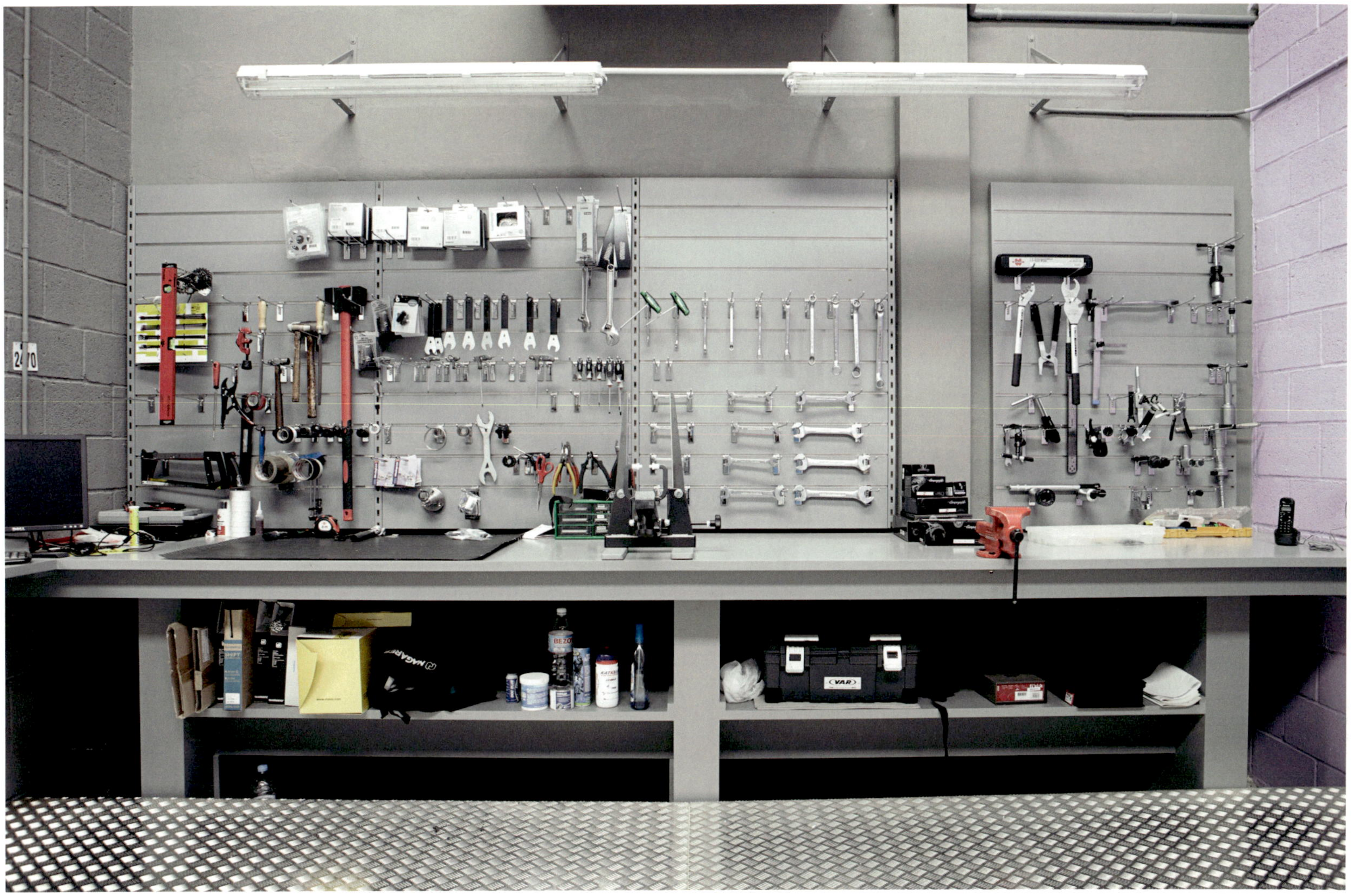

1

ROAD RACER

2

PASSONI

Offering a very special Italian ride, Passoni has been creating bespoke luxury road bicycles since Luciano Passoni founded the company in the early 1980s. Creating exclusive bicycles out of titanium, carbon, and stainless steel, the boutique bicycle manufacturer near Milan is dedicated to a customized, personal approach, using Holistic Bike Fitting to determine the optimal geometrics for each customer. Upholding the family business and the fine heritage of Italian bike building are Passoni owners Silvia Passoni and Matteo Cassina. Cassina credits Silvia Passoni as being a driving force behind the brand in a male-dominated industry, sharpening its image to focus on minimalism, subtlety, and exquisite detail.

1 *TOP GENISIS* 2 *XXTi*

NO IDEA ? — X

GREAT IMAGERY

CADENCE / DKLEIN *ELITE CYCLING KIT*
Founded in San Francisco in 2003 by former bicycle messenger Dustin Klein, Cadence specializes in lifestyle cycling apparel and accessories that explore "boundaries between functionality, concept, and cycling." Cadence began as a one-man operation with Klein doing everything from sewing to shipping. During a three-year hiatus in Seattle, Klein initiated Fast Friday, a monthly cycling event that helped bring together and foster the city's fixed gear cycling community. Cadence might owe part of its success to Klein's cult status in the West Coast cycling scene, but its international growth is testament to a vision that has successfully evolved into a solid brand concept.

RITTE CYCLES Spencer Canon created Ritte Cycles backwards. He first decided to make a cycling kit for himself and his friends. The design didn't seem complete without a team name, which he found in the winner of the 1919 Tour of Flanders. Arriving straight from the war front, Henri "Ritte" Van Lerberghe entered the tour on a borrowed bike. He had such a lead that he stopped at a pub before going on to win the race. Canon was inspired by this spirit of cycling and fun. The popularity of his Ritte kit led him to start a real company. The first Ritte bike was a competitively priced high-end carbon frame from a manufacturer in Taiwan that Canon and his team assembled and branded in their Santa Monica, California studio. The brand became so successful that Ritte now produces in-house custom bikes as well.

1 CROSSBERG

2 1919TT

1

2

Vittoria
CORSA EVO CX 23-28"
cinelli

cinelli
Ken
CAMPAGNOLO
WARNING

ROAD RACER

Previous page
CINELLI *LASER VIVA* Cinelli has reissued its legendary Laser track bike from the 1980s in a number of variations over the years. Now the aerodynamic bike is back in carbon, maintaining the original's geometry with its smoothly sculpted, "webbed" joints, iconic lower fin below the bottom bracket, internal cable routing, and signature metallic blue finish.

KIRSCHNER BRASIL
SANTA CATARINA

While Santa Catarina may still be more known for its surfing, Kirschner is working hard to put the region and Brazil as a whole on the map as a great place to cycle. The new Brazilian cycling apparel brand launched with a line of high end jerseys celebrating its hometown Santa Catarina, with plans to expand the clothing line and produce additional inspiring content and events. Its iconic logo developed with UK creative consultancy Six evokes cycling along the open road through Brazilian terrain, and the Brazilian flag. Combining modern styling with vintage nuances, the unique brand design celebrates the pedigree at the root of the sport.

BERNARD. *CYCLING KIT/SERIES NO. 319*

Brandon Sincock brought together two of his passions—cycling and design—to realize his cycling kit under the brand bernard. When he's not competing in cylocross competitions, Sincock shuttles between Seattle and Los Angeles, working as a freelance art director, photographer, and designer specializing in interactive and motion graphics.

CHRIS KING
CIELO

Based in bicycle mecca Portland, Oregon since 2003, veteran bicycle frame and components manufacturer Chris King is legendary for the precision, quality, and durability of the cycle headsets, hubs, bottom brackets, and tools he has produced since the early 1980s. Until recently, it was less known that he was also a passionate and successful frame builder. Now, 28 years after his first road frames were used by racers and →

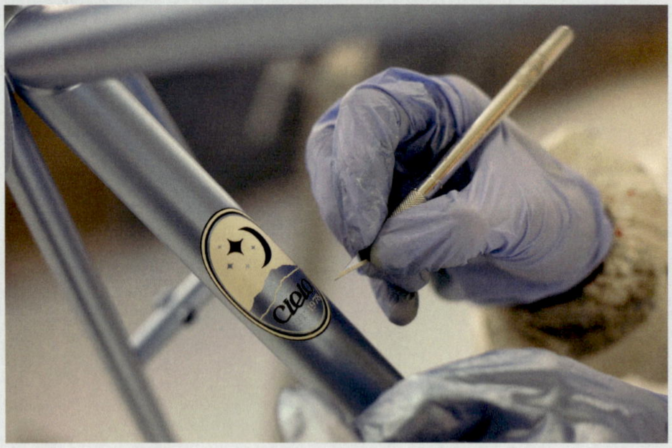

→ non-racers alike, King has revived Cielo Cycles—named for Camino Cielo, "Sky's Pathway," a narrow and adventurous road that runs along the mountains above his native Santa Barbara, California. The handmade, limited run stainless steel framesets come in a variety of standard sizes and include elements designed exclusively for the Cielo frames by Chris King Components. ◇

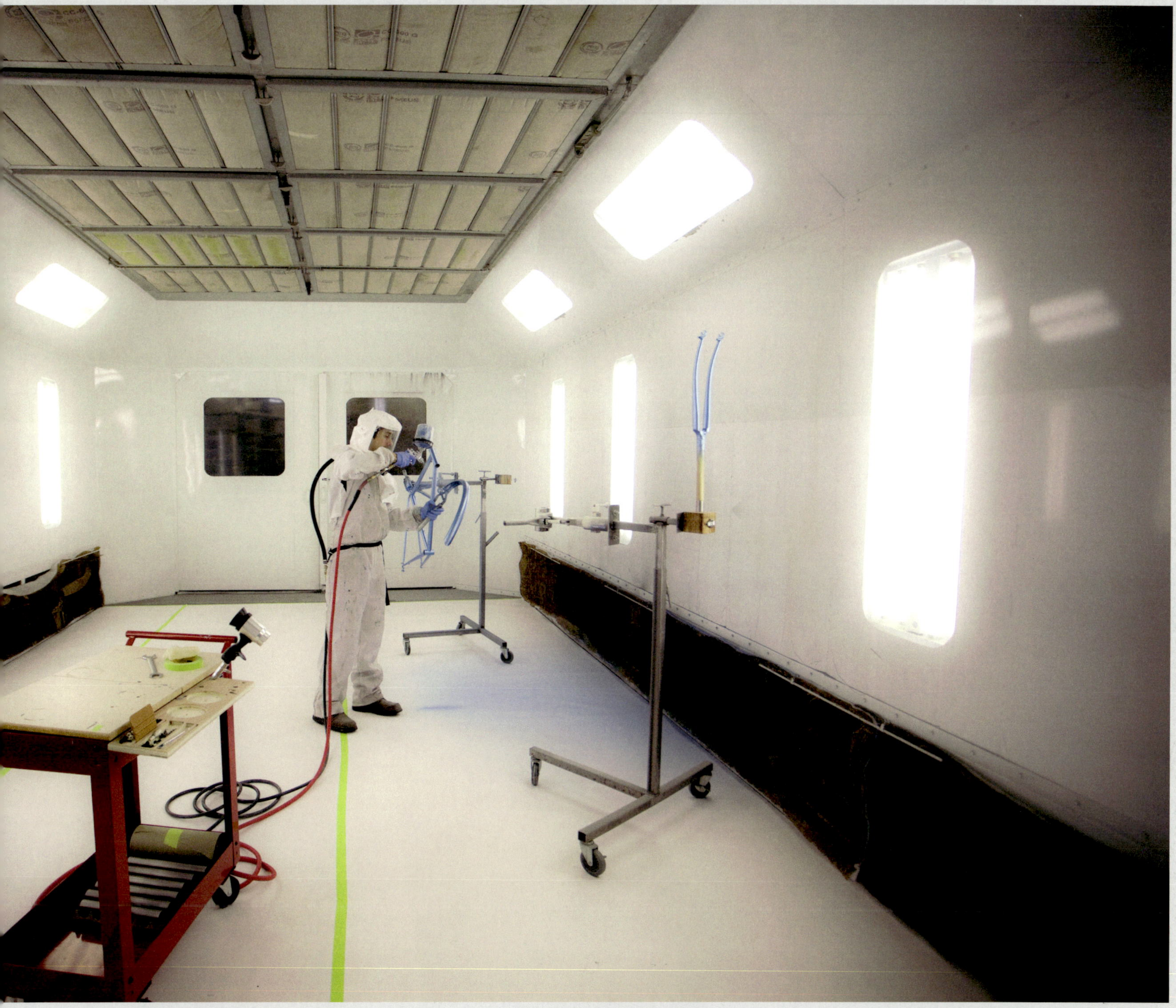

ANDY MARTIN STUDIO
THONET BENTWOOD CONCEPT BIKE

Practically raised on the northern beaches of Sydney, industrial designer and architect Andy Martin "shaped" his first chair at the age of 18, using the same methods as a surfboard designer. In 2010, his 12-year-old London studio, which draws on the skills of craftspeople, furniture and product designers, as well as "futurists," was commissioned by legendary bentwood chair company Thonet to design a limited-edition road bicycle. He was asked to use the same low-tech methods that Michael Thonet developed to build furniture during the 1830s—and then apply them to a highly-engineered 21st-century bike.

In recent years, wooden cycles have experienced a surge in popularity. There are plenty of wooden bikes out there made with varying degrees of elegance and cunning—Ross Lovegrove's bamboo bike, Arndt Menke's shock-absorbing Holzweg, the Waldmeister, the plywood Empira and the Lagomorph, Michael Cubbage's flat frame bike and the flat-packing Greencycle-Eco, the solid oak South African OKES, the timber-framed Russian Xylon, and Jan Gunneweg's asymmetrical, wood-rimmed two-wheeler with natural-tone tires. Andy Martin's remarkable design, however, handsomely illustrates the fact that people outside of the bike community proper, are increasingly passionate about, involved with, and designing bicycles today, not just those "born into," or steeped in, bike culture. Martin's bikes, beautiful in their own right, have the virtue of also being distinctly Thonet: impossibly graceful and reassuringly strong.

Wood is more rigid pound-for-pound than Kevlar, fiberglass, and steel and has extraordinary structural efficiency; Martin made the most of the material. Circumventing the constraints imposed by hand-bending the beech frame (a second model was made using a single piece of hickory), the final jointing and contours of the bike were cut and adjusted on a CNC machine. Martin developed a series of connectors and sprung rods to reinforce its joints and the frame's worst stress points. The delicate-looking seat that crowns that frame has a core of solid beech and is supported on sprung rods while the wheels (not of Martin's design) boast carbon fiber HED H3s.

Martin designed the Thonet to be a fixed gear, brakeless bicycle (though it does have several interchangeable gear ratios). Fixies, as they are affectionately called, have become increasingly beloved because riders say they connect them better to both the bike and the road beneath its wheels. Incidentally, this also makes it strong, lightweight, and low-maintenance, too—the most sophisticated and fashion-forward "seat" that Thonet has steam-bent in 170 years.

1

1
CALFEE DESIGN *BAMBOO TANDEM* Craig Calfee pioneered the use of carbon fiber for bicycle frames in the 1990s; now he has done the same with bamboo. The custom-made bamboo bicycles and frames by the California-based bicycle builder combine artisanal expertise, advanced engineering, and low-carbon manufacturing. Not only is the fast growing bamboo an eco-friendly resource, as a construction material it is lightweight, durable, and amazingly strong. According to Calfee, his bamboo frames offer the ideal combination of stiffness (for efficient transfer of power) and comfort, providing an even smoother ride than aluminum, steel, titanium, and most carbon frames. The bamboo tubes are smoked and heat treated to prevent splitting and held together by hemp fiber lugs. The entire frame is sealed with satin polyurethane.

2
JAN GUNNEWEG *RACING BICYCLE*

2

KEN STOLPMAN *OWEN*

A boatbuilder by trade, Michigan-based New Zealand native Ken Stolpman applied his passion and expertise for wood to a land-based vehicle. The lightweight fixed gear bike has carbon forks and a frame crafted from American white ash, walnut, mahogany, hickory, and Douglas fir, along with marine grade aluminum. It is bonded with epoxy resin. Stolpmann christened his bike "Owen" in honor of his former teacher, Owen Woolley, who was known in his time for building high quality cruising and racing yachts.

STANISŁAW PŁOSKI *BONOBO*

Inspired by Alvar Aalto's iconic sculpted armchairs, Copenhagen-based, Polish designer Stanisław Płoski created Bonobo. With a strong aesthetic marked by clear lines, playful color contrast, and functional components such as a single-gear drive train and hydraulic disc brakes, the low-maintenance bike is designed for the urban rider. Bonobo utilizes wood's inherent properties to absorb shock for a smooth and stylish ride through the city.

GUMA

1

2

JAN GUNNEWEG

Dutch designer Jan Gunneweg is passionate about wood. Following his first wooden hybrid bike in 2004, he went on to make a racing bike in the same year that carried him through several national races. Currently operating from his workshop in Alkmaar, he crafts bespoke bikes from the likes of walnut, ash, French oak, and cherry wood; a larger scale, lower priced wooden bicycle line is in planning.

1
THE HUMAN BIKE
2
BOUGH BIKE
3
HYBRID BICYCLE

3

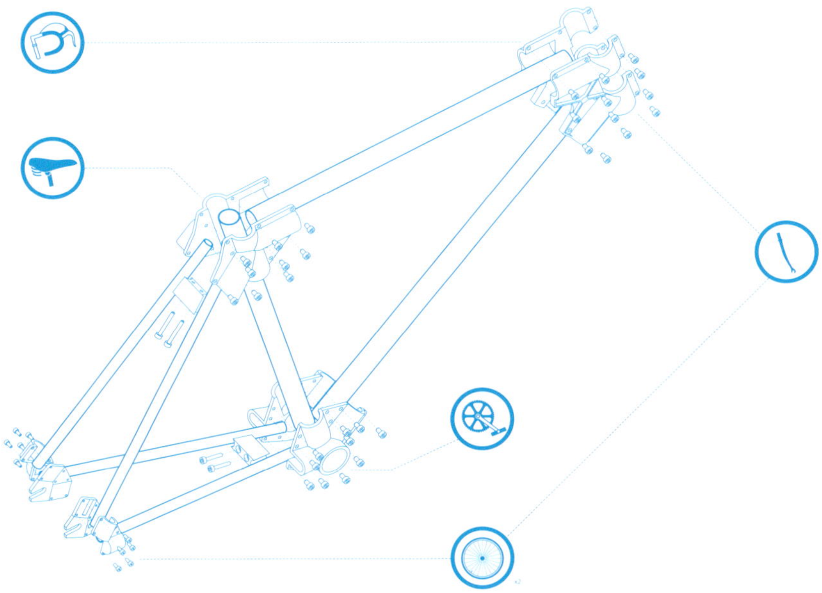

TRISTAN KOPP *PRODUSER*

Kopp's inclusive view of cycling extends to his prodUser platform, a set of connection parts designed to help you build your own bicycle. A manual explaining the additional steps and elements needed to complete the bicycle accompanies the kit. An online proUser platform is being planned, where members can compare their DIY bikes.

HADI TEHERANI
ELECTRONIC BIKE

The e-bike by German architect Hadi Teherani is a push bicycle, produced in a limited edition of 200 pieces, with an electric motor that can be switched on and off. Teherani tucked a rechargeable accumulator battery into an easily removable, black handlebar bag, integrated not just a speedometer but an iPhone cradle into the cockpit navigation, and cleverly concealed the connection between the bag and the switchable e-mode hub motor that he mounted to the front wheel. The lithium-ion battery, which can be detached for recharging at home or in the office as conveniently as, say, a smart phone, has a range of up to 40 km—not bad for a battery so inconspicuous. All in all, Teherani's scheme renders the technology invisible and brings clean good looks to the fore.

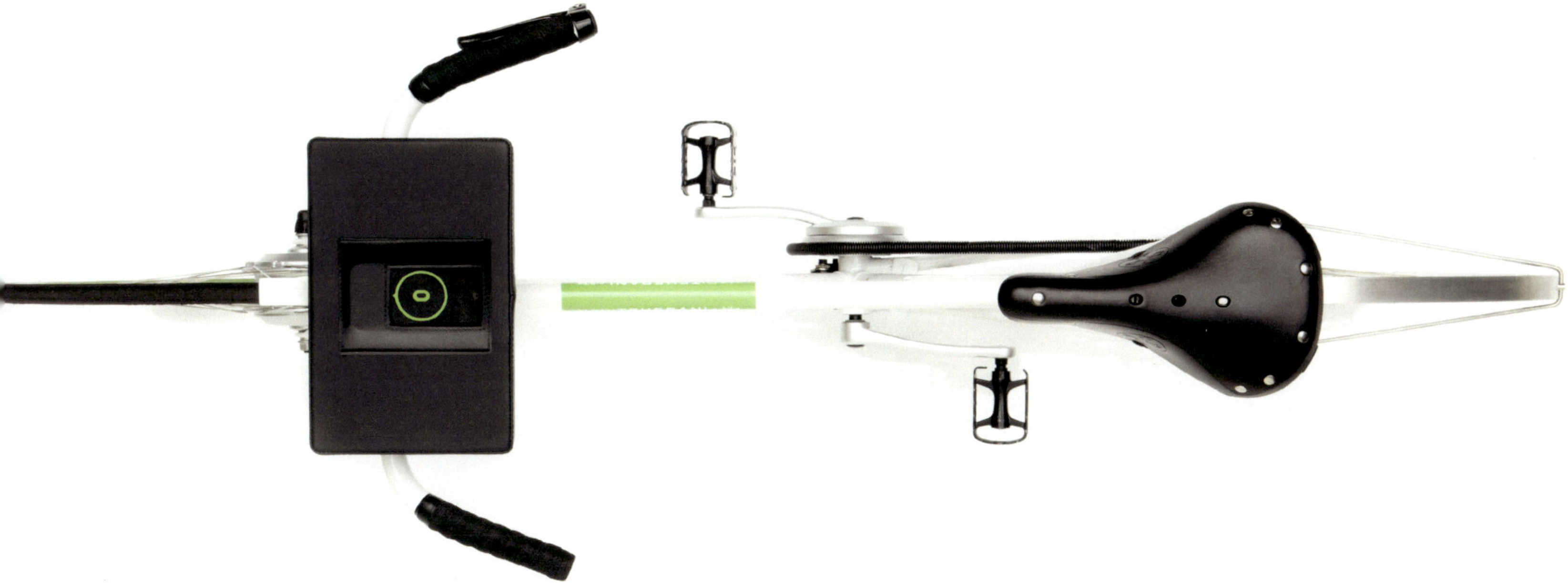

Generally, however, electric bicycles aren't quite so pretty. They are workhorses, not fillies and can travel anywhere between 24 to 32 km per hour and from 7 km uphill on electric power to 70 km along flat roads. The concept is over a century old: In December 1895, Ogden Bolton, Jr. won a patent for a battery-powered bicycle with a DC hub motor mounted to the rear wheel that drew up to 100 amperes from a 10-volt battery. Within two years, Boston's Hosea W. Libbey had filed U.S. Patent 596,272 for a bicycle driven by a "double electric motor" that was set in the hub of the crankset axle.

About 120 years later, e-bike usage across the globe is growing rapidly. By 2010, the Chinese were riding an estimated 120 million e-bikes while sales were also booming in India, America, the Netherlands, and Switzerland. In Europe, as a whole, sales more than trebled in the three years starting from 2007. Good news, because, environmentally, electric and human-powered hybrid bicycles are considered to be 18 times more energy efficient than an SUV, six times more efficient than rail transit, and may have only as much impact on the planet as a conventional bicycle.

So why don't most e-bikes look as fashionable as conventional ones? Teherani's does. And no wonder. On his website, the designer looks dapper in a rather unbuilder-like white suit. He was born in Tehran, schooled in Hamburg and started his career as a fashion designer in Cologne before turning to architecture. Today, he has offices in Moscow, Dubai, and Hamburg. Teherani has said that he was looking to create not just a technically sophisticated machine, but something "classic, functional, timeless, sustainable, and unique." But also stylish: The white sport-lugged CroMo steel frame features a leather Brooks saddle, one green rim and one white, and a sporty, minimalist sensibility that appears as visually and technologically "light" as it is lightweight.

FARADAY BICYCLES *PORTEUR*

Riders have the option of busting a sweat or enjoying an easy glide up San Francisco's hilly terrain in classic elegance on the Faraday Porteur. The prototype designed by a team led by Faraday founder Adam Vollmer won the Oregon Manifest design challenge to construct "the ultimate modern utility bike" in 2012 and following a successful campaign on Kickstarter went into its first production soon after. The bike has a retro-style frame in white and seafoam green with leather trim and bamboo fenders. The hidden lithium-ion battery pack and 250-watt motor provide 16 to 24 km of assisted pedaling in boost mode and can be recharged in about 45 minutes. LED lights switch on automatically in dark conditions and the frame mounted cargo rack carries up to 14 kg. The bike itself weighs about 20 kg.

Faraday

Faraday

1

1
36 VOLT:
EINARNMIGER BANDIT
2
36 VOLT: VORRADLER

2

ELECTROLYTE *36 VOLT*

Matthias Blümel, Martin Meier, and Sebastian Wegerle of Electrolyte in Germany united their passion for cycling with the fun and practicality of assisted acceleration in their line of e-bikes aptly named 36 Volt. The sporty, lightweight, handcrafted frames made of aluminum or titanium and carbon in the deluxe versions are discretely outfitted with a small 250-watt hub motor powered by a 1.3 kg, 36-volt battery. Additional weight is spared by the absence of a gearshift. Pushing the turbo button on the handlebar activates the motor; otherwise the e-bike functions as an ordinary, single speed bicycle. The battery will take you about 15 km at a maximum of 25 km/h and only while pedaling–due to German legal restrictions and the team's belief that "cycling is more fun than riding scooters."

1

HASE
BionX
PINO
hasebikes.com
SCHWALBE
MARATHON PLUS

2

SCHWALBE

3

1
HASE BIKES *PINO*
2
ELECTROLYTE *36 VOLT: BÜROHENGST*
3
ELECTROLYTE *36 VOLT: BRANDSTIFTER*
4
ELECTROLYTE *36 VOLT: STRASSENFEGER*

4

PG-BIKES

PG-Bikes CEO Manuel Ostner has long had an eye for extravagant bicycles. At age 22 he co-founded the Pimp Garage in Regensburg, offering extravagantly individualized two-wheelers. The cult shop led to an MTV series. After a financial fiasco forced him into bankruptcy, Ostner rose from the ashes with PG-Bikes, producing luxury, lifestyle oriented e-bikes, pedelecs, and urban bikes. The products of their collaboration with Christian Zanzotti of UBC, the Blacktrail 1 and 2, are allegedly the world's most expensive e-bikes (60,000 euros and 100,000 euros, respectively). PG-Bikes also has a more moderately priced e-bike, along with an innovative braided-carbon fiber bicycle, created with Munich Composites. With endorsements by Lady Gaga and Orlando Bloom, Ostner is clearly aiming for international cult appeal.

blacktrail™

INDEX

A

B

C

D

E

F

RIVENDELL BICYCLE WORKS
www.rivbike.com

Pages 188–191

ROBERT WECHSLER
www.robertwechsler.com
Photography: Robert Wechsler

Page 158

S

SHAPE FIELD OFFICE
www.shape-sf.com
Design: Nicholas Riddle
Photography: Curtis Myers

Pages 98–99

SINT CHRISTOPHORUS
www.sintchristophorus.nl
Design, photography: Michiel van den Brink

Page 39

SIZEMORE BICYCLE
www.sizemorebicycle.com
Design, photography: Taylor Sizemore

Page 100 (#2)

SKEPPSHULT
www.skeppshult.se
Design: Björn Dahlström
Photography: Patrik Johäll

Pages 144–145

SPURCYCLE
www.spurcycle.com

Page 30

STANISŁAW PŁOSKI
www.stanislawploski.com
Photography: Stanisław Płoski,
Piotr Antonów (page 228)

Pages 228-229

STANRIDGE SPEED
www.stanridgespeed.com
Design: Adam Eldridge
Photography: David Sigler

Page 147

STEVEN NERERO | SINGLE APE
www.singleape.com
Photography: Steven Nereo

Pages 27, 165

SWIFT INDUSTRIES
www.builtbyswift.com
Design: Martina Brimmer
Photography: Russ Roca

Pages 181

T

TERRY RICARDO
terryricardo.tumblr.com
Client: Melbourne Bikefest

Page 65

TINO POHLMANN
www.t-pohlmann.de
Client: Eintausend Magazine
Photography: Tino Pohlmann

Pages 34–35

TOKYOBIKE
www.tokyobike.com

Pages 6, 40–43

TRISTAN KOPP
www.tristankopp.com
Design, photography: Tristan Kopp,
Gaspard Tiné-Berès – www.gaspardtineberes.com
(Mamalova – page 174-175)
Photography: Tristan Kopp
Thanks to: Ricardo Carneiro, Lou Rihn,
Claire Fumex
(prodUSER – page 232)

Pages 174-175, 232-233

TRUE UNIQUE
www.trueunique.de
Client: Mifa Universal
Design: Manuel Dulz
Photography: Manu
(Transport Fuchs – page 131)
Photography: Stefan Rechsteiner
(Wooden 2-Track – page 96)

Pages 96–97, 131

TSUNEHIRO CYCLES
www.tsunehirocycles.com
Client: Dana Hayes / Tsunehiro Cycles
Design: Rob Tsunehiro
Photography: Anna M. Campbell
(Grocery Getter – page 117),
Client: Oregon Manifest Design Challenge,
Silas Beebe ID+
Design: Rob Tsunehiro, Silas Beebe
(Oregon Manifest Midtail - page 184 #1)

Pages 117, 184 (#1)

U

UBC
www.ubc-coren.com
Design: Christian Zanzotti

Page 207

UGO GATTONI
www.ugogattoni.fr
Client: Nobrow
Photography: Pierre-Luc Baron-Moreau

Page 148

ULTRACICLI
www.ultrabox.it
Photography: Marco Martelli

Pages 46–47

V

W

Y

Pier 84

VELO
2ND GEAR

BICYCLE
CULTURE
AND
STYLE

This book was edited and designed by Gestalten

Edited by Sven Ehmann and Robert Klanten
Preface and features by Shonquis Moreno
Project texts by Alisa Kotmair

Cover and layout by Kasper Zwaaneveld
Cover photography by Tino Pohlmann, model: Medea Paffenholz
Typefaces: Ovink by Sofie Beier, Bonesana Pro by Matthieu Cortat
Foundry: www.gestaltenfonts.com

Project management by Pauleena Chbib
Production management by Martin Bretschneider
Proofreading by Bettina Klein
Printed by Optimal Media GmbH, Röbel
Made in Germany

Published by Gestalten, Berlin 2013
ISBN 978-3-89955-473-1

2nd printing, 2013

For more information, please visit www.gestalten.com.

Bibliographic information published by the Deutsche Nationalbibliothek.
The Deutsche Nationalbibliothek lists this publication in the Deutsche Nationalbibliografie; detailed bibliographic data are available online at http://dnb.d-nb.de.

None of the content in this book was published in exchange for payment by commercial parties or designers; Gestalten selected all included work based solely on its artistic merit.

This book was printed according to the internationally accepted ISO 14001 standards for environmental protection, which specify requirements for an environmental management system.

This book was printed on paper certified by the FSC®.

FSC www.fsc.org MIX Paper from responsible sources FSC® C108521

Gestalten is a climate-neutral company. We collaborate with the non-profit carbon offset provider myclimate (www.myclimate.org) to neutralize the company's carbon footprint produced through our worldwide business activities by investing in projects that reduce CO_2 emissions (www.gestalten.com/myclimate).

myclimate
Protect our planet

COLORADO
PRO-MIYATA

RALEIGH
LECOULANT
CYCLES
MERCIER

HANEBRINK